Amitabha Buddha

Artist: Chiang, Yi-tze

Collection of the National Palace Museum,
Taipei, Taiwan. Republic of China

2

If you recite the Buddha's name,
reciting without cease,
The mouth recites "Amita"
and makes things of a piece.
Scattered thoughts do not arise,
Samadhi you attain.
For rebirth in the Pure Land,
you hope is not in vain.

Collection of the National Palace Museum,
Taipei, Taiwan. Republic of China

When one recites
"Namo Amitabha Buddha,"
in the Western Land of Ultimate Bliss,
in one of the pools of the seven jewels
filled with the eight waters of merit
and virtue, a lotus flower grows.
The more one recites,
the bigger it grows,
but it won't bloom until the end of life,
when one's self-nature goes to
be reborn in it.

Amitabha Buddha is contained within the hearts of
all living beings and living beings
are contained within Amitabha's heart.
In that way phenomena and noumenon mesh.
So have faith in the doctrine
and energetically practice it by reciting
the Buddha's name more and more every day.

Reciting the Buddha's name
gets rid of discursive thought.
One who recites the name all day long
will have no discursive thought.
The absence of such thought is wonderful.
The wonderful Dharma purges us of
greed, hate, and stupidity.

Faith, vows, and practice are the
three prerequisites for cultivation
of the Pure Land Dharma Door.
First, believe there is a Land of Ultimate Bliss.
Secondly, have faith in Amitabha Buddha.
Thirdly, believe that you and Amitabha Buddha
have a great karmic affinity, and
that you can certainly be born in
the Land of Ultimate Bliss.

There's no need to do anything else;
it's easy, simple, and convenient.
It doesn't cost a thing,
and yet this method is the highest
and most supreme, for if we just recite,
"Namo Amitabha Buddha,"
we can be born in the Land of Ultimate Bliss.

When you achieve the third,

Real Mark recitation, even if you try,

you cannot stop reciting the Buddha's name.

The recitation flows like water and lives within you.

This is the state of the Buddha-recitation samadhi:

reciting and yet not reciting,

not reciting and yet reciting.

When something happens, a wise one reflects;
When it passes, he is still.

Everywhere according with conditions
as the years and months go by,
he nonetheless minds his own business
in any given moment.

If we see affairs and are awake,
We can transcend the world.
If we see affairs and are confused,
We will fall into rebirth once again.

What is the origin of the dharma-doors?

The Buddhas spoke all dharmas for
the minds of people.
If there were no minds,
what use would dharmas be?

Saying, "Namo Amitabha Buddha"
creates a Buddha-thought in our mind.
When we are mindful of the Buddha,
the Buddha is mindful of us.
It's like communication by radio or radar.
We recite here, and it's received there.
But if we don't recite, nothing is received;
so we must hold and recite the name.

The Land of Ultimate Bliss

is the original true heart and mind of us all.

Uncovering and discovering this heart,

helps us be born in the Land of Ultimate Bliss.

Until we understand our own true heart

we won't get there.

The Land of Ultimate Bliss is within our hearts,

not outside.

The Venerable Master Hsuan Hua

The Buddha Speaks of
Amitabha Sutra

The Buddha Speaks of Amitabha Sutra

A General Explanation

with commentary by the

Venerable Master Hsuan Hua

English translation by the
Buddhist Text Translation Society

Buddhist Text Translation Society
Dharma Realm Buddhist University
Dharma Realm Buddhist Association
Burlingame, California U.S.A.

The Buddha Speaks of Amitabha Sutra
A General Explanation

Published and translated by:

Buddhist Text Translation Society
1777 Murchison Drive, Burlingame, CA 94010-4504

© 2003   **Buddhist Text Translation Society**
         Dharma Realm Buddhist University
         Dharma Realm Buddhist Association

First edition (USA) 1974
Second edition (USA) 2003

12 11 10 09 08 07 06 05 04 03   10 9 8 7 6 5 4 3 2 1

ISBN 0-88139-431-9

Printed in Taiwan.

Addresses of the Dharma Realm Buddhist Association branches are listed at the back of this book.

Library of Congress Cataloging-in-Publication Data

Hsüan Hua, 1908-
    The Buddha speaks of Amitabha Sutra : a general explanation / with commentaries of the Venerable Master Hsuan Hua ; English translation by the Buddhist Text Translation Society.
        p. cm.
Includes index.
    ISBN 0-88139-431-9
    1. Tripiéaka. Sëtrapiéaka. Sukhavativyëha
(Smaller)--Commentaries. I. Buddhist Text Translation Society. II. Title.

BQ2047 .H785 2003
294.3'85--dc21
                                              2002012935

Contents

Introduction

by Tripitaka Master Hsuan Hua

The *Buddha Speaks of Amitabha Sutra* belongs to the class of sutras spoken without formal request. It describes in detail the supremely beautiful adornments of the Western Land of Ultimate Bliss. Living beings of the ten directions need only recite Amitabha Buddha's name, practicing even just the Dharma of Ten Recitations, in order to be assured of rebirth in that land.

When the Buddhadharma becomes extinct in the Saha World, this sutra will be the last to disappear. The first to go will be the *Shurangama Sutra*, the sutra most feared by heavenly demons and other religions, all of whom would like to see every existing copy of it burned to ashes. The *Shurangama Sutra* catches the reflections of the "li mei" and "wang liang" ghosts who, unable to hide, hate it with vengeance. Scholars who are without sufficient common sense fall in with the demons. This is truly pitiable.

The *Buddha Speaks of Amitabha Sutra* may be compared to a great magnet, and the living beings of the ten directions are like iron filings; all the filings, without exception, are drawn to the magnet.

Now, upon the completion of the English translation, I have added these words as a brief introduction.

Why You Should Read This Book

Gold Mountain Shramana Tripitaka Master Hua explains the path of self-cultivation as it has never been explained before.

Where other Buddhist Masters merely recite texts, the Venerable Master illuminates the Way so that those who hear are crystal clear about its meaning. Where other Buddhist Masters explain texts with the intellectual juggling of manifold lists and technical discriminations which easily confuse an audience, the Venerable Master picks out the essentials which reveal the methods to eradicate suffering. Where other Buddhist Masters repeat interpretations learned by rote, the Venerable Master speaks directly to the conditions around him, showing one man how to free himself from the grip of arrogance and conceit, instructing another how to relieve the suffering of chronic illness; showing one how to shake off the bonds of heavy emotional attachments, instructing others on the way to recover from the pain of loss; showing one how to be patient and peaceful in the face of slander, scoldings, and beatings; showing others how, ultimately, to put an end to the unbroken cycle of birth and death. To the degree that those who seek his instruction are capable of understanding, to that degree the Venerable Master explains the Dharma, showing those of limited understanding how to be free from the suffering of excessive greed and anger, or how to transform stupidity into wisdom, and guiding those whose capacity is great to put an end to the last traces of birth and death. Never trapped in convention, the Venerable Master's teaching covers the whole spectrum, leading beings from the hells, through all the intermediate realms of mind, and establishing them in the wonderful enlightenment of Buddhahood.

Where scholars worry about sources and chronology, discriminate the goods and bads of secondary sources, and try to organize an attendant host of biographical and bibliographical minutiae, the Venerable Master deals directly with the ultimate meaning of the primary texts. Although he teaches with unassuming simplicity, when he speaks people spontaneously change for the good and come to understand the profound and mysterious. His teaching is so thorough that it affects everything, but none of those who seek his instruction leans on him. When he seems to be doing nothing, his influence is felt everywhere, and when no one is aware of him, he fills everyone with happiness. His teaching transcends teaching.

How is it that he has come to be able to teach in a way that is so unlike the ways of others? It is because he has cultivated the path to enlightenment and has arrived at the goal that what he says can be believed. This is what makes him different from everyone else who talks about self-cultivation, and this is why you should read this book.

You may wonder about the particulars of his cultivation of the Way. There is much too much to present here, and so a general summary will have to suffice.

Tripitaka Master Hsuan Hua (also named An Ci and Duo Lun) was born on the sixteenth day of the third month, lunar calendar, in 1908. His father, Bai Fu-hai was a farmer in the Shuang-cheng District of Northeastern China. The Master was the youngest of eight children. His mother often recited the name of Amitabha Buddha, and in a dream one night shortly before the Master was born, she saw Amitabha Buddha emitting a light which illumined the entire world. When she awoke, her room was filled with a rare fragrance.

Because the Master's home was in the countryside where there were few people, he did not become aware of death until he was eleven years old. When he did, it stunned him. While walking with some friends in a pasture, he came upon the body of a dead baby. The Master did not understand why the baby was lying still on the ground and asked his friends, who simply said, "She's dead." Puzzled, he returned home and asked his mother what exactly death was. "All people, whether rich or poor, must die," she said, "either from old age, sickness, or accidentally."

"How does one free oneself from death?" the Master asked insistently.

At that time there was a visitor in his home who answered the Master's question by saying, "It is only through cultivation of the Way, awakening to one's own mind and seeing one's fundamental nature that one can gain liberation from the continous cycle of birth and death in the six paths."

On hearing this the Master wished immediately to leave the home-life and begin cultivation, but his mother told him that he must wait, for she needed him to care for her in her old age. He complied with her wishes, serving both his parents with the greatest devotion; his filial piety earned him the name "Filial Son Bai." He did, however, take refuge with the Triple Jewel, bowing to the Venerable Master Chang Zhi as his teacher.

Although the Master had but a few years of formal schooling, he is extremely well-educated. Possessed of a photographic memory, he was able to memorize the Four Books and the Five Classics of Chinese literature in an amazingly short time. Moreover, in addition to his mastery of the Buddhist Canon, he is well versed in the study of medicine, physiognomy, and astrology.

When he was nineteen years old his mother died. After receiving the shramanera precepts from his master, he took up the practice of sitting by his mother's grave, observing a mourning period of three years. He lived in an A-frame hut made from sorghum stalks where he cultivated dhyana samadhi and recited the name of Amitabha Buddha, ate only one meal a day, and never lay down to sleep. Occasionally he would enter samadhi for weeks at a time, never rising from his seat.

One night the residents of the nearby village saw that the Master's hut was on fire. A blazing light shot up into the air for some ten yards, making the area around the hut as bright as broad daylight. Many people rushed to the graveyard, shouting as they went, "The filial son's hut has caught fire!" and soon there were hundreds of people there to lend assistance with buckets of water. When they arrived, however, they found the hut unburned; the Master was sitting absorbed in meditation.

On one occasion, the Sixth Patriarch, Great Master Hui Neng of the Tang dynasty, came to the Master's hut and told him that in the future he would go to the West where he would meet many people with whom he had affinities and thereby establish the Dharma, causing it to flourish. After the Second World War the Master travelled three thousand miles to Nan Hua Monastery in Canton Province to pay his respects to the Venerable Master Hsu Yun, who was then one hundred and nine years old. During his journey he resided at Pu Tou Mountain, the Bodhimanda of the Bodhisattva Avalokiteshvara, where he received the complete bhikshu precepts. When he arrived at Nan Hua the two masters greeted one another; the Venerable Master Hsu Yun recognised the Master's attainment and transmitted the wonderful mind seal to him, making him the Ninth Patriarch of the Wei Yang Lineage, and asked him to serve as the Director of the Nan Hua Institute for the Study of the Vinaya.

In 1950 he resigned his post at Nan Hua Monastery and journeyed to Hong Kong where he lived in a mountain side cave in the New Territories. He stayed in the cave until the large influx of Sangha members fleeing the mainland required his help in establishing new monasteries and temples throughout Hong Kong. He personally established two temples and a lecture hall and helped to bring about the construction of many others. He dwelt in Hong Kong for twelve years, during which many people were influenced by his arduous cultivation and awesome manner to take refuge with the Triple Jewel and support the propagation of the Buddhadharma.

In 1962 he carried the Buddha's Dharma banner farther west to the shores of America where he took up residence in San Franscisco and patiently waited for past causes to ripen and bear their fruit. In the beginning of the year 1968 the Master declared that the flower of Buddhism would bloom that year in America with five petals; in the summer of that year the Master conducted the Shurangama Sutra Dharma Assembly which lasted 96 days – five of the people who attended that session left the home-life and became bhikshus and bhikshunis under the Master's guidance. Since that time the Master has conducted many Dharma assemblies, and delivered lectures on the *Heart Sutra*, the *Diamond Sutra*, the *Sixth Patriarch's Sutra*, the *Amitabha Sutra*, the *Sutra of the Past Vows of Earth Store Bodhisattva*, the *Great Compassion Heart Dharani Sutra*, and the *Dharma Blossom Sutra*. In June 1971 the Master commenced a Dharma Assembly on the king of sutras, the *Avatamsaka Sutra*. With such tireless vigor the Master has firmly planted the roots of Dharma in western soil so that it can become self-perpetuating. He has spent many hours every day explaining the teachings and their application in cultivation, steeping his disciples in the nectar of Dharma that they might carry on the Buddha's teaching.

The miraculous events that have taken place in the Master's life are far too numerous to relate in this brief sketch. He has freed many from the burdens of disease and other afflictions, and his followers number in the tens of thousands. His steadfast cultivation of bitter practices, the moral prohibitions, and the six paramitas, paired with his unwavering samadhi and profound knowledge of the teachings serve as a model for living beings throughout the entire dharmarealm.

Disciple Guo Jan
Gold Mountain
June, 1974.

Translator's Introduction

Shakyamuni Buddha spoke the *Amitabha Sutra* to let all living beings know of the power of Amitabha Buddha's great vows to lead all who recite his name with faith to rebirth in his Buddhaland, the Land of Ultimate Bliss, where they may cultivate and quickly realize Buddhahood.

Of the five great schools of Buddhism – the Chan (Zen) School, the Teaching School, the Vinaya School, the Secret School, and the Pure Land School – the Pure Land Dharma door of Buddha-recitation is the most suited for living beings of the Dharma-ending Age, when beings are beset by external disasters and internal obstacles. It is extremely direct and encompasses beings of all dispositions.

For a true understanding of the *Amitabha Sutra*, the explanation of the Venerable Master Hsuan Hua is indispensable. In the fall of 1969, the Master delivered a series of lectures to his American disciples, brilliantly revealing the essence of the Pure Land Doctrine and causing his American listeners to bring forth deep and sincere faith in the practice of the Pure Land. The lectures were tape-recorded and have now been transcribed so that students of the Dharma everywhere may study them, put them into practice, and thus be filled with the joy of Dharma.

The Venerable Master Hua, through the power of his vows and vast compassion, has come to the West, carrying the mind-seal of all Buddhas as it has been passed in succession from Shakyamuni Buddha, through Patriarch Bodhidharma, the Great Master the

Sixth Patriarch Hui Neng, through the Venerable Master Hsu Yun who in turn transmitted the Dharma to the Venerable Master Hua. Thus, the Master is the 46th Patriarch from Shakyamuni Buddha, the 18th Patriarch in China from Bodhidharma, the Ninth Patriarch of the Wei Yang Lineage, and the First Patriarch in the West.

The Master's creed:

Freezing, we do not scheme.
Starving, we do not beg.
Dying of poverty, we ask for nothing.
We accord with conditions, but do not change.
We do not change, yet accord with conditions.
These are our three great principles.

We renounce our lives to do the Buddha's work.
We take molding our destinies as our basic duty.
We rectify our lives to do the Sangha's work.
In our actions we understand the principles,
So that our principles are revealed in our actions.
We carry out the pulse of
the Patriarchs' mind-transmission.

If you wish to comprehend the profound principles found within the sutras, it is essential that you attend Dharma Assemblies and hear the sutras explained by qualified teachers. The Venerable Master Hua's untiring vigor in lecturing on the Dharma is unmatched. He has resolved that as long as he has a single breath of air, he will continue to elucidate the sutras, regardless of how many people come to listen. If there is only one person, or when there are hundreds, he lectures just the same. At Gold Mountain Monastery, the Dharma is explained every day, seven days a week, 365 days a year. Such intensive lecturing is unparalleled in the entire history of Buddhism in the world.

On June 17, 1968, at the Buddhist Lecture Hall in San Francisco, the Master began a series of lectures on the *Shurangama*

Sutra to a group of 40 university students during a 96-day Sutra Study and Meditation Session. Each lecture took a minimum of two hours to deliver and translate. When it became evident that the sutra was too long to finish on schedule, the Master began lecturing twice a day, once in the afternoon and once in the evening, and then three times a day, adding a lecture in the mornings. Finally, by the end of the summer, the Master was lecturing four times a day. The session ended on September 22, 1968.

Following the *Shurangama Sutra* session, the gathering of disciples grew steadily. Many who had come from Seattle, Washington to attend the session took up permanent residence in San Francisco, drawn like filings to a magnet to the forthcoming Lotus Sutra assembly which formally began November 10, 1968. The Master delivered lectures nightly on the sutra. Two years, and over 350 lectures later, the assembly was concluded on November 10, 1970.

Shakyamuni Buddha taught the Dharma for 49 years, in over 300 Assemblies, and left limitless Dharma treasures in the world. He taught 84,000 dharma doors to counteract people's 84,000 kinds of afflictions. The Master has labored to expose students to the fullest possible range of the Buddha's teaching. Thus, on November 16, 1968, he began expounding the *Sutra of the Past Vows of Earth Store Bodhisattva* at weekly Saturday afternoon lectures which continued regularly until September 22, 1969.

At the request of his disciples, the Master also began lecturing the *Diamond Sutra* weekly on Sunday afternoons. The series ran from November 17, 1968 to April 6, 1969. No sooner had he finished lecturing the *Diamond Sutra*, than he agreed to explain the *Heart Sutra* with his *Verses Without a Stand*. That series ran from April 20, 1969 to July 27, 1969. As soon as the *Heart Sutra* assembly was concluded, many eager disciples requested an explanation of the *Great Compassion Heart Dharani Sutra* which began on August 3, 1969 and ended on January 18, 1970.

The second annual Summer Session began on June 16, 1969. During the session the Master lectured daily in the afternoons on the *Chapter on the Conduct and Vows of Samantabhadra*, from the *Avatamsaka Sutra*, in addition to nightly lectures on the *Dharma Flower Sutra*. When the Chapter was finished on July 25, 1969, he then explained the *Sixth Patriarch's Dharma Jewel Platform Sutra* daily from August 4, 1969 to September 12, 1969.

The Master's tireless dedication inspired deep faith and unwavering vigor in his disciples. Consequentially five of them went to Asia where they received the full ordination in Keelung, Taiwan, and returned as America's first Bhikshus and Bhikshunis. In their absence the *Dharma Flower Sutra* lectures were replaced by nightly lectures on the *Amitabha Sutra* which ran from October 29, 1969 to December 25, 1969. *Dharma Flower Sutra* lectures resumed in January, 1970, after one of the numerous intensive Chan Meditation and Buddha Recitation Sessions hosted by the Master at which he delivered lively and informative talks daily. The number of disciples continued to grow. Between May 17 and June 7, 1970, the Master delivered lectures on the *Shastra to the Door of Understanding the Hundred Dharmas*. The third annual Summer Session in 1970 revolved around lectures on the *Dharma Flower* which continued until autumn when the Assembly came to a close. At that time the Great Hundred Day Meditation Session was inaugurated. The session consisted of fourteen straight weeks of Chan meditation, from three o'clock in the morning until twelve midnight, beginning on November 15, 1970. The Master delivered nightly lectures on the *Records of Eminent Monks* (*gao seng zhuan*) along with meditation instruction. As usual, the Master continued to lecture in the afternoons on weekends, making a total of nine lectures weekly. During this period the Master also founded Gold Mountain Monastery and supervised its construction. The Sino-American Buddhist Association took up headquarters there. On April 18, 1971, the Master began weekly Sunday lectures on the *Awakening of Faith in the Mahayana Shastra*.

On June 13, 1970, the first day of the fourth annual Summer Session, the Master began lecturing on National Master Qing Liang's preface to the *Great Avatamsaka Sutra*. The Master lectured National Master Qing Liang's prologue to the *Avatamsaka* as well. Lecturing daily for a year and five months, he finished, 375 lectures later, on November 10, 1972. On November 12, 1972, the Master inaugurated the Great Avatamsaka Assembly, expounded it daily, sometimes as often as nine times a week. It took nine years to complete that lecture series.

Following the completion of the Avatamsaka series, the Master agreed to the disciples' respectful request that he explain the Shurangama Mantra. The Master used original verses to explain the lines of mantra, and then commented upon the lines and the verses. This extraordinary series is unprecedented. The Master also explained several chapters of the *Nirvana Sutra*. This is but a brief outline of how the Master has worked with selfless devotion to lay the foundation of the Buddha's teaching on Western soil.

The Dharma itself has no orthodox, resemblance, or Dharma-ending Age; it is living beings who create the distinctions. One who cultivates the Orthodox Dharma lives in the Orthodox Dharma Age and will obtain the orthodox enlightenment. In the *Amitabha Sutra*, the Buddha says, "Shariputra, if there are people who have already made the vow, who now make the vow, or who are about to make the vow, 'I desire to be born in Amitabha's country,' these people, whether born in the past, now being born, or to be born in the future, all will irreversibly attain Anuttarasamyaksambodhi." The Master's commentary presents a most rare opportunity to study the principles of the Pure Land, and those who have faith, who make vows, and who actually practice this dharma-door are assured of a miraculous response.

Disciple Guo Yi
Buddhist Text Translation Society, June 25, 1974.

The Land of Ultimate Bliss

Who would not like to end all suffering and enjoy every bliss? This new translation tells exactly how it can be done. The *Buddha Speaks of Amitabha Sutra* which sets forth the methods leading to birth in the Land of Ultimate Bliss, the Western Paradise of the Buddha Amitabha, first appeared in the *Vajra Bodhi Sea*. A complete translation of the *Amitabha Sutra* from the Chinese text was printed in issue nine, and a Sanskrit language lesson based upon its Sanskrit text appeared in each issue; and this translation of the Venerable Master Hua's explanation was first published there. What had been lacking was a full explanation of just what this sutra is about gathered in one place for ready reference by students of the Way.

The practice of mindfulness and recitation of the Buddha's name is widespread in the Orient, but even there only rarely is it fully understood and cultivated. How much the more so is that true in the West, where the recollection of the Buddha's name, if known at all, is generally mistaken for an ecstatic devotional cult. Such a view is a great mistake and results from a misunderstanding of the basic principles of Buddhism, for recitation of the Buddha's name is actually an inconceivably wonderful dharma door that includes all other Buddhist practices. Now at last there has appeared the authoritative explanation of this sutra text, translated from the lectures of the Most Venerable High Master Hua, which clarifies this dharma door and reveals the profound depths to which this mindfulness of the Buddha extends.

Bhikshuni Heng Hsien, Ph.D.

The Translation of the Text

The present translation is of the small *Sukhavati-vyuha*. Two sutras, the large and the small, have this title, both taking as subject Amitabha Buddha, his pure Buddhaland to the West, and the means to rebirth therein. *Sukhavati*, or, as translated from the Chinese, Ultimate Bliss, is the name of this land. A third sutra also describes Sukhavati: the *Amitayurdhyana-sutra*. Together, these three comprise the basic texts of the Pure Land Sect. The translated text, the small Sukhavati-vyuha, although it is the shortest of the three, is by no means unimportant. Nor is it just a summary recapitulation of the doctrine set forth in the other two. The large Sukhavati-vyuha explains the causal connections resulting in the Pure Land of Ultimate Bliss. It deals with Amitabha's vows of former lives and their realization in Sukhavati. The *Amitayurdhyana-sutra* is concerned with quite another matter. It is a guide to cultivation and describes a series of sixteen meditations which lead to various grades of transformational rebirth in Sukhavati. Summaries of both sutras are readily found in the literature and so are not given here.

Both sutras contain Dharmas preached in specific response to the requests of sentient beings: the large Sukhavati-vyuha at the request of Ananda, "who had still to be advanced on the path of disciples"; the *Amitayurdhyana-sutra* at the request of Vaidehi, queen mother of the wicked Prince Ajatasatru:

> *"My only prayer," she continued, "is this: O World Honored One, mayest thou preach to me in detail of all the places where there is no sorrow or trouble, and where I ought to go to be born anew. I am not satisfied with this*

world of depravities, with Jambudvipa which is full of hells,
full of hungry ghosts (pretas), and of the brute creation. In
this world of depravities there is many an assemblage of the
wicked. May I not hear, I pray, the voice of the wicked in the
future; and may I not see any wicked person."

The small Sukhavati-vyuha, in contra-distinction, is unique because the entire sutra belongs to the "self-spoken" division. In other words, the Buddha himself spontaneously preached the Dharma, overstepping the usual practice of speaking Dharma on request. The very fact that no one in the Great Assembly knew to ask shows the extreme importance and inconceivability of this specific Dharma. Thus, the Buddha clearly warns, "You should know that I, in the evil time of the five turbidities... for all the world speak this Dharma, difficult to believe, extremely difficult."

The original draft of the translation was made as a text to be used in conjunction with the spontaneous oral translations of Tripitaka Master Hsuan Hua's sublime lectures on this sutra. It was felt that an accurate and fairly literal translation was needed to do justice to the subtleties of the commentary.

Afterwards, it was decided to chant the sutra as part of the daily activities at the Buddhist Lecture Hall. In order to produce an English version suitable for chanting, some revision of the literal translation was necessary; however, great care has been taken to preserve the meaning, even at the cost of "chantability." Although the product is a long way from Kumarajiva's pristine clarity, it is hoped that a step has been made in that direction. And perhaps with growing familiarity and cultivation, progress will be rapid.

Ronald B. Epstein, Ph.D.
September 1st, 1974.

釋迦牟尼文佛

Namo Original Teacher Shakyamuni Buddha

Verse for Opening a Sutra

The unsurpassed, profound, and wonderful dharma,
Is difficult to encounter in hundreds of millions of eons,
I now see and hear it, receive and uphold it,
And I vow to fathom the Tathagata's true meaning.

PART I

THE FIVE-FOLD PROFOUND MEANINGS

According to the instructions of the Tian Tai School, sutras are outlined according to Five-fold Profound Meanings: Explaining the Name, Describing the Substance, Clarifying the Principle, Discussing the Function, and Determining the Teaching Mark. The Five-fold Meanings are called "five-fold" because they unfold, layer after layer.

Explaining the Name

The first is Explaining the Name. Only when you know the sutra's name can you begin to understand its principles. Just as when you meet a person you first learn his name, so it is with sutras, for each has its own particular name.

The titles of all Buddhist sutras may be divided into two parts, the common title and the special title. The special title of this sutra is the *Buddha Speaks of Amitabha*, and the word sutra is the common title, as all discourses spoken by the Buddha are called sutras.

Although five kinds of beings may speak sutras,

1) The Buddhas,
2) The Buddha's disciples,
3) Gods,
4) Immortals, and
5) Transformation beings, that is, gods or Buddhas who transform into human form.

The disciples, gods, immortals, and transformation beings must first receive the Buddha's certification before they speak a sutra; without certification, what they speak is not truly a sutra. This sutra was spoken by the Buddha, not by those in the other four categories; it came from Shakyamuni Buddha's mouth.

Because its principles were too profound and wonderful for the Sravakas or Bodhisattvas to comprehend, no one requested the Pure Land dharma-door. Nonetheless, it had to be revealed and so the Buddha spontaneously spoke this very important sutra, doubly important because it will be the last to disappear in the Dharma-ending age.

In the future, the Buddhadharma will become extinct. Demon Kings most fear the Shurangama Mantra and so the *Shurangama Sutra* will be the first to disappear, for without the sutra, no one will be able to recite the mantra. Then, one by one, the other sutras will disappear. We now have the black words of the text on white paper, but in the future, when the Buddhadharma is on the verge of extinction, the words will disappear from the page, as all the sutras vanish. The last to go will be the *Amitabha Sutra*. It will remain in the world an additional hundred years and ferry limitless living beings across the sea of suffering to the other shore, which is Nirvana. When the *Amitabha Sutra* has been forgotten, only the great phrase "Namo Amitabha Buddha" will remain among mankind and save limitless beings. Next, the word "Namo" which is Sanskrit and means "homage to" will be lost, and only "Amitabha Buddha" will remain for another hundred years, rescuing living beings. After that, the Buddhadharma will completely disappear from the world. Because this sutra will be the last to disappear, it is extremely important.

The Special Title : *The Buddha Speaks of Amitabha*

Who is the Buddha? The Buddha is the Greatly Enlightened One. His great enlightenment is an awakening to all things, without a particle of confusion. A true Buddha has ended karma and transcended emotions. He is without karmic obstacles and devoid of emotional responses. On the other hand we find living beings, who are attached to emotions and worldly love. Common men with heavy karma and confused emotions are simply living beings. The Buddha's enlightenment may be said to be of three kinds:

1) Basic enlightenment, enlightenment at the root source
2) Beginning enlightenment, the initial stages of enlightenment, and
3) Ultimate enlightenment, complete enlightenment.

You can also say that he is

1) Self-enlightened, that he
2) Enlightens others, and that he is
3) Complete in enlightenment and practice.

Self-enlightenment. Common men are unenlightened. They
think themselves intelligent when they are actually quite dull. They
gamble thinking that they will win – who would have guessed that
they'd lose? Why are they so confused? It's because they do things
which they clearly know are wrong. The more confused they are,
the deeper they sink into confusion; the deeper they sink, the more
confused they become.

Everyone should become enlightened. The Buddha is a part of
all living beings and is one of them himself, but because he is
enlightened instead of confused, he is said to be self-enlightened
and not like common men. Sravakas, the disciples of the Small
Vehicle, are "independents"; they are self-enlightened, but they do
not enlighten others.

Bodhisattvas enlighten others, unlike the Sravakas who think
only of themselves. Bodhisattvas choose to benefit all beings and
ask for nothing in return. Using their own methods of self-enlightenment, they convert all beings causing them to realize the doctrine
of enlightenment and non-confusion. This is the practice of the
Bodhisattva conduct.

Sravakas, "sound-hearers", awaken to the Way upon hearing
the sound of the Buddha's voice. They cultivate the Four Holy
Truths,

1) Suffering,
2) Origination,

3) Extinction, and

4) The Way.

They also cultivate the Twelve Causes and Conditions:

1) Ignorance, which conditions

2) Action, action which conditions

3) Consciousness, consciousness which conditions

4) Name and form, name and form which conditions

5) The six sense organs, the six sense organs which condition

6) Contact, contact which conditions

7) Feeling, feeling which conditions

8) Craving, craving which conditions

9) Grasping, grasping which conditions

10) Becoming, becoming which conditions

11) Birth, and birth which conditions

12) Old age and death.

The twelve all arise from ignorance, and ignorance is merely a lack of understanding. Without ignorance, the Twelve Causes and Conditions cease to operate. But if you flounder in ignorance, you are caught in the remaining causes. Those of the Small Vehicle cultivate the Dharma, but Bodhisattvas transcend all successive stages, cultivating the Six Perfections and the Ten-thousand conducts.

The Six Perfections are:

1) Giving. Giving transforms those who are stingy. Greedy people who can't give should practice giving, for if they do not learn to give they will never get rid of their stinginess.

2) Morality. The precepts are guides to perfect conduct and eliminate offenses, transgressions, and evil deeds. Keep the precepts.

3) Patience. Patience transforms those who are hateful. If you have an unreasonable temper, cultivate being patient and bearing

with things. Don't be an asura, a fighter who gets angry all day and is not on speaking terms with anyone unless it's to speak while glaring with fierce, angry eyes. Be patient instead.

4) Vigor. Vigor transforms those who are lazy. If you're lazy, learn to be vigorous.

5) Dhyana meditation. Dhyana meditation transforms those who are scattered and confused.

6) Wisdom. Prajna wisdom transforms those who are stupid; the bright light of wisdom disperses the darkness of stupidity.

Bodhisattvas cultivate the Six Perfections and the Ten-thousand conducts. Self-enlightened, they enlighten others, and are therefore unlike those of the Small Vehicle.

Complete Enlightenment. This is wonderful enlightenment, the enlightenment of the Buddha. The Buddha perfects self-enlightenment and the enlightenment of others, and when his enlightenment and practice are complete, he has realized Buddhahood.

"You keep talking about the Buddha," you say, "but I still don't know who the Buddha is."

You don't know? I will tell you.

You are the Buddha.

"Then why don't I know it?" you ask.

Your not knowing is just the Buddha! But this is not to say that you have already reached Buddhahood. You are as yet an unrealized Buddha. You should understand that the Buddha became a Buddha from the stage of a common person. It is just living beings who can cultivate to realize Buddhahood. The Buddha is the Enlightened One, and when a human being becomes enlightened, he's a Buddha, too. Without enlightenment, he's just a living being. This is a general explanation of the word "Buddha."

The Buddha has Three Bodies, Four Wisdoms, Five Eyes, and Six Spiritual Penetrations. You may be a Buddha, but you are still an unrealized Buddha, for you do not have these powers. The

Buddha cultivated from the stage of a common person to Buddhahood, and has all the attributes of Buddhahood.

Some who haven't become Buddhas claim to be Buddhas. This is the height of stupidity; claiming to be what they are not, they cheat themselves and cheat others. Isn't this to be a "Greatly Stupid One?" Everyone can become a Buddha, but cultivation is necessary. If one has the Three Bodies and the Four Wisdoms one may call oneself a Buddha. If one has just the Five Eyes, or a bit of spiritual penetration, one may not.

The Three Bodies are:

1) The Dharma body,
2) The Reward body,
3) The Transformation body.

The Four Wisdoms are:

1) The Great Perfect Mirror Wisdom,
2) The Wonderful Observing Wisdom,
3) The Wisdom of Accomplishing What is Done, and
4) The Equality Wisdom.

The Six Spiritual Penetrations are:

1) The Heavenly Eye. The Heavenly Eye can see the gods and watch all their activities.
2) The Heavenly Ear. The Heavenly Ear can hear the speech and sounds of the gods.
3) The Knowledge of Others' Thoughts. Thoughts in the minds of others which they have not yet spoken are already known. This refers to the present.
4) The Knowledge of Past Lives. With this penetration one can also know the past.
5) The Extinction of Outflows. To be without outflows is to have no thoughts of greed, hate, stupidity, or sexual desire. In general, once one gets rid of all one's bad habits and faults, one has no outflows. Outflows are like water

running through a leaky bottle; at the stage of no outflows the leaks have been stopped up.

6) The Complete Spirit. Also called the Penetration of the Spiritual Realm, this is an inconceivably wonderful state.

The Five Eyes are:

1) The Heavenly Eye,
2) The Buddha Eye,
3) The Wisdom Eye,
4) The Dharma Eye, and
5) The Flesh Eye.

A verse about the Five Eyes says,

The Heavenly Eye penetrates without obstruction.
The Flesh Eye sees obstacles but does not penetrate.
The Dharma Eye only contemplates the mundane.
The Wisdom Eye understands True Emptiness.
The Buddha Eye shines like a thousand suns.
Although the illuminations differ,
Their substance is one.

The Heavenly Eye penetrates without obstruction and sees the affairs of eighty-thousand great aeons. It cannot see beyond that. The Flesh Eye can see those things which are obstructed; the Heavenly Eye only sees those things which are not obstructed. The Dharma Eye contemplates the "mundane truth", all the affairs of worldly existence. The Wisdom Eye comprehends the state of True Emptiness, the "genuine truth."

Not just the Buddha, but everyone has a Buddha Eye. Some have opened their Buddha Eyes and some have not. The open Buddha Eye shines with the blazing intensity of a thousand suns. Although the Five Eyes differ in what they see, they are basically of the same substance.

So the Buddha has Three Bodies, Four Wisdoms, Five Eyes, and Six Spiritual Penetrations. If one has such talent, one may call oneself a Buddha, but if not, one would be better off being a good person instead of trying to cheat people.

In this sutra, Shakyamuni Buddha, the teacher of the Saha world, speaks of the adornments of the Land of Ultimate Bliss and of its teacher, Amitabha Buddha.

Saha is a Sanskrit term which mean "to be endured."[1] The world in which we live has so much suffering that living beings find it hard to endure, and so it is named Saha.

Shakyamuni Buddha's name, also Sanskrit, is explained in two parts. Sakya, his family name, means "able to be humane."[2] The Buddha shows his humaneness as compassion which relieves suffering, and kindness which bestows happiness by teaching and transforming living beings.

There are three kinds of compassion:

1) An Attitude of Loving Compassion.

Average men love and sympathize with those close to them, but not with strangers. Seeing relatives or friends in distress, they exhaust their strength to help them, but when strangers are suffering, they pay them no heed. Having compassion for those you love is called an Attitude of Loving Compassion.

There is as well an Attitude of Loving Compassion which extends to those of the same species, but not to those of other species. For example, not only do people have no compassion for animals such as oxen, pigs, chickens, geese, or ducks, but they even go so far as to eat animals' flesh! They snatch away animals' lives in order to nourish their own. This is not a true Attitude of Loving Compassion. Fortunately, people rarely eat each other. They may eat pork, mutton, beef, chicken, duck, and fish, but they don't

---

[1.] *kan ren* 堪忍
[2.] *neng ren* 能仁

catch, kill, and eat each other, and so they are a bit better off than animals that turn on members of their own species for food. People may not eat each other, but they certainly have no true Attitude of Loving Compassion towards animals.

2) Compassion which comes from understanding conditioned dharmas.

Those of the Small Vehicle have compassion which comes from understanding conditioned dharmas as well as the attitude of loving compassion discussed above. They contemplate all dharmas as arising from causes and conditions and they know that:

Causes and conditions have no nature;
Their very substance is emptiness.

Contemplating the emptiness of conditioned dharmas, they compassionately teach and transform living beings without becoming attached to the teaching and transforming. They know that everything is empty.

3) The Great Compassion which comes from understanding the identical substance of all beings.

Buddha and Bodhisattvas have yet another kind of compassion. The Buddha's Dharma body pervades all places and so the Buddhas and Bodhisattvas are of one substance with all beings; the Buddha's heart and nature are all-pervasive and all beings are contained within it. We are living beings within the Buddha's heart and he is the Buddha within our hearts. Our hearts and the Buddha's are the same, everywhere throughout the ten directions, north, east, south, west, the directions in between, above, and below. Therefore the Buddha and living beings are of the same substance, without distinction. This is called the Great Compassion.

Sakya, the Buddha's family name, includes these three kinds of compassion. If one chose to speak about it in more detail, there are limitless and unbounded meanings.

Muni is the Buddha's personal name. It means "still and quiet."[3] Still and unmoving, he is silent. No words from the mouth, no thoughts from the mind – this is an inconceivable state. The Buddha speaks Dharma without speaking; he speaks and yet does not speak, does not speak and yet he speaks. This is still and silent, still, still, silent and unmoving, yet responding in accord; responding in accord and yet always, always silent and still. This is the meaning of the Buddha's personal name, Muni. All Buddhas have the name Buddha in common, but only this Buddha has the special name Shakyamuni.

Continuing the explanation of the title, we shall now investigate the meaning of "speak." In Chinese, the word speak 說 *shuo* is made up of the radical 言 *yan* which means "word," and the element 兌 *dui*. Dui has two dots ˅ on the top which were originally the word 人 *ren*, person. The strokes below 儿 could also represent the word person.

The words... 言

of one man's... ˅

mouth, said to... 口

another man... 儿

make up the word "speak"... 說

What does the Buddha say? Whatever he pleases, but happy to say what he wants to say, he always speaks the Dharma.

Having already become Buddhas, Shakyamuni Buddha and the Buddhas of the ten directions are called "already enlightened ones," as they have already understood and awakened from their dreams. While we are still sound asleep and dreaming, the Buddha is greatly

---

3. *ji mo* 寂默

enlightened, greatly awakened. With his Buddha-wisdom there is nothing he does not know; using his Buddha-vision there is nothing he does not see. This is the meaning of his great enlightenment which came from cultivating, and this is the result to which he has certified. He has walked the road, he has been through it, he is an "already enlightened one." The methods of cultivation he used to attain the fruit of enlightenment he then teaches, to lead all living beings to attain and certify to that ultimate, complete result of Bodhi. That is why he speaks the Dharma, and why, having done so, he is happy to have spoken.

What does he say?

Right now he speaks of Amitabha: the *Buddha Speaks of Amitabha Sutra.*

Amitabha, the next word in the title, is a Sanskrit word which means "limitless light."[4] Amitabha's other name, Amitayus, means "limitless life."[5]

"But," you might ask, "the sutra says that it has been ten kalpas since Amitabha realized Buddhahood. Ten kalpas is a definite length of time. Why do you speak of 'limitless life' and then measure it out in time?"

Amitayus, "limitless life," refers to his blessings and virtue. "Limitless light" refers to his wisdom. His wisdom light is limitless and bright. Limitless life, limitless light. Not only are his blessings, virtues, and wisdom limitless but so are his spiritual powers, his eloquence, his attributes, and his teachings. There is no way to count them because they are infinite, nowhere present and nowhere absent.

Where did the limitless come from? Mathematicians should know that the limitless comes from the one. One is many and many are one. A scholar once wrote a book and said, "Large numbers are

---

[4.] *wu liang guang* 無量光, from the Sanskrit *amita,* "unmeasured" and *abha,* "splendor, light."

[5.] *wu liang shou* 無量壽, from the Sanskrit *amita* and *ayus,* "life-span, life."

written by starting with one and then employing many place holding zeros. Keep adding zeros until the space between heaven and earth is filled. When you have written all over your walls and covered your floors, can you determine the total? Couldn't you still add another zero? Numbers are endless."

Amitabha Buddha's life, wisdom, merit, virtue, and Way-power are all infinite and unbounded. If you want a big figure, go ahead and write columns of zeros.

Knowing that there can be no definite total, the Buddha, who is the perfection of intelligence, just said, "Limitless and uncountable." Mathematics can explain infinity, and scientists have sent men into space to study it, but having arrived in empty space, there's still more empty space beyond. There's no end to it. Numbers go on infinitely and in this way we can understand the vast expanse of Amitabha Buddha's blessedness, his virtue, and his wisdom. Therefore he is called Amita.

Both Amitabha and Shakyamuni Buddha were people who became Buddhas. They did not descend from the heavens or ascend from the depths of the earth. As people they cultivated the Dharma and now they are sages, people who have realized the result. According to the classification of sutra titles, this sutra is established by reference to a person, but not a person like us. He is a Buddha, one who has realized the result. We are living beings; we have not realized the result, but are cultivating the cause of Buddhahood. Once Buddhahood is realized, we will be sages. This sage's name, Amitabha, is used to classify the title of the sutra.

The Common Title : *Sutra*

A sutra is called a "tallying text."[6] It tallies with the wonderful principles of all Buddhas above and with the opportunities for teaching living beings below. Each time I explain a sutra, I add more meanings to the word. If I told you all of the meanings at

---

6. *ji qing* 契經

once, you would never remember them, or if you did, the next time I spoke about it you would say, "I know all about it, a sutra strings together, attracts, is permanent, and is a method. The Master certainly is repetitious." So I explain the term "sutra" bit by bit. In this commentary on the *Amitabha Sutra* I will discuss five of its meanings:

1) Basic Dharma. The Buddha reveals the origin of Dharma with his teaching by means of Four Kinds of Complete Giving:

a) Mundane Complete Giving, using ordinary methods of expression,

b) Curative Complete Giving, curing each living being of his particular problem,

c) Complete Giving that is for everyone, teaching for the sake of all living beings,

d) The Complete Giving of the Primary Meaning, giving the highest principle to all beings.

Ultimately, the Dharma cannot be spoken because there is no Dharma to speak; but by practicing the Four Kinds of Complete Giving, the Buddha reveals it. Thus the word sutra has the meaning of Basic Dharma.

2) Subtle Dharma. Unless the profound and wonderful doctrines are elucidated in the sutras, no one can know of them.

3) Bubbling Spring. Principles flow from sutras like gushing water from artesian wells.

4) Guideline. To make guidelines, ancient carpenters and stonemasons used a string covered with black ink, held the string taut, pulled it up, let it snap and made a straight, black line. A sutra is also like a compass and square, used for guiding people.

5) A Garland. The principles are linked together in the sutras like flowers woven into a garland.

The word sutra also has four additional meanings:

1) Strings Together. Sutras string together the principles of the Buddhadharma.

2) Attracts. Sutras attract living beings who are in need of the teaching.

3) Method. The methods used in cultivation which have been employed from ancient times right up until the present are set forth in the sutras.

4) Permanent. Sutras are permanent and unchanging; not one word can be left out or added to them, and heavenly demons and non-Buddhist religions cannot harm them.

The word sutra also means "a path." If you wanted, for example, to go to New York and didn't know the way, you might run west instead of east. You could run all your life, but you would never get to New York. Cultivating is also like this. Unless you know the road, you may practice forever, but will never arrive at Buddhahood.

Sutras are also a canon, fixed documents to rely upon when cultivating according to Dharma. Sutras also explain worldly dharmas. You can find any doctrine you wish in the sutras.

Sutras are everyone's breath; without them men are lost. We should step outside of our stuffy rooms to breathe the fresh air of the sutras. People can't live without air or sutras.

You ask, "I don't study sutras or the Dharma, so I don't breathe that air, do I?"

Your breathe it, too, because the Dharma air fills the world, and whether or not you study it, you breathe it all the same. Everyone shares the air. Students of the Buddhadharma exhale Buddhadharma air and non-students breathe it in. You can't avoid this relationship.

Sutras are also food for the spirit, and have many uses. When you're melancholy or depressed, recite sutras, for they explain the doctrines in a wonderful way, which dispels your gloom and opens your heart.

Sutra is the common name of all sutras; this sutra's particular name is the *Buddha Speaks of Amitabha*. There are many sutra names, because the Buddha left limitless unbounded Dharma-jewels in the world; but of these hundreds and thousands of sutras, none go beyond the Seven Classifications.

The Seven Classifications of Sutra Titles

In order to clarify their content, sutra titles are divided into seven types by their reference to person, dharma, and analogy.

1) Single Three. Three of the seven titles are established by reference to either person, dharma, or analogy.

a) The *Buddha Speaks of Amitabha Sutra*[7] refers only to people. Shakyamuni Buddha and Amitabha Buddha are both people who cultivated and became Buddhas.

b) The *Great Parinirvana Sutra*[8] is an example of a title classified by reference to a dharma. Nirvana is the dharma of non-production and non-extinction.

c) The *Net of Brahma Sutra*[9] is a title established only by reference to analogy, the analogy of the net of the Great Brahma King. The net in the Brahma heaven has many holes in it, like a fish net, and there is a gem in every hole. Each gem radiates more brilliantly than an electric light and they shine upon each other – light shines upon light, reflected through the interstices of the net. They inter-illumine, without conflict. One light, for example, would never say to another, "I hate your light, lamp. It's terrible! I'm the only one who can shine around here." Lamps don't fight with each other like people.

[7.] *fo shuo a mi tuo jing* 佛說阿彌陀經, *Sukhavativyuha-sutra*

[8.] *da bwo nie pan jing* 大般涅槃經, *Mahaparinirvana-sutra*

[9.] *fan wan jing* 梵網經, *Brahmajala-sutra*

The net of Brahma is an analogy for the precepts. Each precept is like a gem, and those who have left home are one of the Three Jewels because they keep the precepts purely. Members of the Sangha cultivate to have no improper thoughts concerning their environment. Thus they transcend the material world, attain purity, and shine like gems in the net of Brahma.

2) Double Three. Titles established by reference to a combination of either person and dharma, person and analogy, or dharma and analogy are called "double three."

d) The *Sutra of Questions of Manjushri*[10] is a title established by reference to a person, the greatly wise Bodhisattva Manjushri, and the Dharma he requested, Prajna. Only the most intelligent Bodhisattva knew to ask about the meaning of Prajna. One of great wisdom requesting the dharma of great wisdom classifies the sutra title according to person and dharma.

e) The *Lion Roar of the Thus Come One Sutra*[11] is a title established by reference to a person, the Thus Come One, and an analogy, the Lion Roar. The Buddha speaks Dharma like the lion roars, and when the King of Beasts roars, the wild beasts tremble. So, in his *Song of Certifying to the Way*, the Great Master Yong Jia wrote,

> *The roar of the lion is the fearless speaking;*
> *When the wild beasts hear it,*
>   *their heads split wide open.*
> *Elephants run wild and lose their decorum,*
> *But gods and dragons, in silence,*
>   *hear it with delight.*

---

10. *wen shu shi li wen jing* 文殊師利問經, *Manjusripariprccha-sutra*
11. *shi ji hou jing* 獅子吼經, *Simhanadika-sutra*

The Buddha speaks the Dharma like the fearless lion roars. When the lion roars, the other animals are frozen with fright. Elephants are usually quite sedate, but they lose their powerful authoritarian stance. Gods, dragons, and the rest of the eight-fold division[12], however, are delighted.

f) The *Wonderful Dharma Lotus Blossom Sutra*[13] is an example of a title established by reference to a dharma and an analogy, since the wonderful Dharma is analogous to a lotus flower.

3) Complete in One. The seventh classification contains references to all three subjects: person, dharma, and analogy.

g) The *Great Means Expansive Buddha Flower Adornment Sutra*[14]. In this sutra, Great, Means, and Expansive refer to the wonderful Dharma of realizing Buddhahood; Flower Adornment is an analogy – the causal flowers of the ten thousand conducts are used to adorn the supreme virtue of the fruit.

The Twelve Divisions of Sutra Texts

In addition to the Seven Classifications of Sutra Titles, the texts comprising the entire Tripitaka, or Buddhist Canon, may be divided into twelve categories:

1) Prose lines.

2) Repetition of the meanings presented in the prose lines in short "verse lines" makes the text easy to remember.

---

[12] The eight-fold division, or eight classes of supernatural beings are: gods, dragons, yaksa ghosts, gandharvas (musical spirits), kinnaras (also musical spirits), asuras (beings who like to fight), garudas (great-golden winged birds), and mahoragas (giant snakes).

[13] *miao fa lian hua jing* 妙法蓮華經, *Saddharmapundarika-sutra*

[14] *da fang guang fwo hua yan jing* 大方廣佛華嚴經, *Mahavaipulyabuddhavatamsaka-sutra*

3) Predictions of Buddhahood. Although future Buddhas have not yet realized Buddhahood, the present Buddha predicts their eventual accomplishment and gives them each a name.

4) Interjections do not fit with the principles which come before or after them. They arise alone, like the short verses in the *Vajra (Diamond) Sutra.*

5) The *Buddha Speaks of Amitabha Sutra* belongs to the category of sutras "spoken without request." The Sound Hearer Disciples were not ready to understand the doctrines of the Pure Land dharma-door, and the Bodhisattvas hadn't conceived of this method or heard of Amitabha's vow to save all beings. Everyone said that reciting the Buddha's name was an old woman's pastime and that those with wisdom did not need to study it. This is a serious mistake because unless you recite the Buddha's name you continue to have useless scattered, lustful, desire-ridden thought. Reciting the Buddha's name gets rid of discursive thought. One who recites the name all day long will have *no* discursive thought. The absence of such thought is wonderful. The wonderful Dharma purges us of greed, hate, and stupidity. When I was seventeen I wrote a verse:

> *The King of all Dharmas is*
> *the one word "Amitabha."*
> *The five periods and the eight teachings*[15]
> *are all contained within it.*
> *One who singlemindedly remembers*
> *and recites his name*
> *Will enter into the still, and bright,*
> *and unmoving field.*

[15.] The *Tian Tai* School divides the Buddha's teachings into five periods: the *Avatamsaka, Agama, Vaipulya, Prajna,* and *Lotus-Nirvana.* The teachings are also arranged in eight categories, four according to methods of teaching: sudden, gradual, secret, and unfixed, and four according to the nature of the teaching: the storehouse teaching, the connecting teaching, the separate teaching, and the perfect teaching.

Reciting the Buddha's name is much better than all of your crazy ideas!

This sutra describes the practices leading to the Buddha's Pure Land. Bodhisattvas didn't ask for this Dharma because they simply did not understand the subtle advantages of reciting the Buddha's name. Since no one asked for this wonderful Dharma, Shakyamuni Buddha spoke without request.

6) Causes and conditions are also spoken by the Buddhas.

7) Analogies.

8) Past events discuss the events in the lives of the Buddha's disciples.

9) Past lives discuss the events in the past lives of the Buddha.

10) Universal writings explain principle in an especially expansive way.

11) New sutras are those which have never been spoken before.

12) Commentaries.

The essential message of this sutra teaches us to recite the name "Namo Amitabha Buddha." Amitabha Buddha has a great affinity with living beings of the Saha world. Before realizing Buddhahood, he made forty-eight vows and each one involved taking living beings to Buddhahood. At that time, he was a Bhikshu named Dharma Treasury. He said, "When I realize Buddhahood, I vow that living beings who recite my name will also realize Buddhahood. Otherwise, I won't either."

This is similar to the vow made by Avalokitesvara Bodhisattva in the *Great Compassion Heart Dharani Sutra*: "If anyone who recites this spiritual mantra does not obtain whatever he seeks, then this cannot be the Great Compassion Dharani."

By the power of his vows, Amitabha Buddha leads all beings to rebirth in his country where they realize Buddhahood. This power attracts living beings to the Land of Ultimate Bliss, just as a magnet attracts iron filings. If living beings do not attain enlightenment, he himself won't realize Buddhahood. Therefore, all who recite his name can realize Buddhahood.

The dharma-door of reciting the Buddha's name receives those of all three faculties and accepts both the intelligent and the stupid. People with wisdom have superior faculties, ordinary people have average faculties, and stupid people have inferior faculties. But whether one is intelligent, average, or stupid, if one recites the Buddha's name one will definitely be born transformationally from a lotus in the Land of Ultimate Bliss. One will not pass through the womb but will enter a lotus flower, live in it for a while, and then realize Buddhahood. Whether you are stupid or wise, you can realize Buddhahood.

You say, "I don't believe you can realize Buddhahood simply by reciting the Buddha's name. It's too easy. It's like borrowing Amitabha's power to realize Buddhahood."

You should not disbelieve this because a long time ago, Amitabha signed an agreement with us which said, "after I realize Buddhahood, you can recite my name and do so as well." Since we signed our names, if we recite, we are sure to become Buddhas.

Furthermore, reciting the Buddha's name establishes a firm foundation and plants good roots. For example, there was once an old man who wanted to leave home. Although he was about seventy or eighty years old, couldn't get around well, and was aware of his impending death, he thought he could easily leave home and be a High Master of Buddhism. When he arrived at the Garden of the Benefactor of Orphans and the Solitary, he found that Shakyamuni Buddha had gone out to receive offerings. His disciples, the Arhats, opened their heavenly eyes and took a look at this man's past causes. Seeing that he hadn't done a single good deed in the past eighty-thousand great aeons, they told him that he couldn't leave home.

When he heard this, the old man's heart turned cold and he ran, thinking, "If I can't leave home, I'll kill myself." Just as he was about to throw himself into the ocean, Shakyamuni Buddha caught him and said, "What are you doing?"

"I wanted to leave home," cried the man, "but the Buddha wasn't at the Garden, and the great Bhikshus told me that I couldn't because I have no good roots. My life is meaningless. I'm too old to work, and no one takes care of me. I might as well be dead."

Shakyamuni Buddha said, "Don't throw yourself into the ocean. I'll accept you."

"You will?" said the man. "Who are you? Do you have the authority?"

Shakyamuni Buddha said, "I am the Buddha, and those Bhikshus are my disciples; none of them will object."

The old man wiped his eyes and blew his nose. "There's hope for me," he said.

The old man's head was shaved. He became a monk and immediately certified to the first stage of Arhatship. Why? When he heard that he couldn't leave home, he had decided to drown himself; although he didn't really die, he was as good as dead. "I've already thrown myself into the sea," he said, and relinquished all his attachment to life. He saw right through everything, won his independence, and certified to the first stage of Arhatship.

This bothered the Bhikshus. "How strange," they murmured, "the man has no good roots. We wouldn't let him leave home, but the Buddha accepted him and now he's certified to Arhatship. People without good roots can't do that. Such a contradiction in the Teaching will never do! Let's go ask the Buddha."

Then they went before the Buddha, bowed reverently, and asked, "We are basically clear-minded. How could that old man without good roots certify to Arhatship? How can the Buddhadharma be so inconsistent?"

Shakyamuni Buddha said, "As Arhats, you see only the events of the past eighty thousand aeons ago. More than eighty thousand aeons ago, the old man was a firewood gatherer. One day in the mountains he was attacked by a tiger and quickly climbed a tree. The tiger leaped and snapped his jaws, but missed.

"This tiger, however, was smarter than the average tiger, 'I'll show you,' it said. 'I'll chew through the trunk of the tree and when it falls I'll eat you.'

"Now, if a mouse can gnaw through wood, how much the more so can a tiger. Tigers can make powder out of human bones. It chewed half way through the tree and terrified the old man whose life was hanging by a thread. Then he remembered, 'In times of danger, people recite the Buddha's name,' and he called out, 'Namo Buddha!' which scared the tiger away and saved his life. After that, the old man forgot to recite, and so on this side of eighty thousand great aeons, he failed to plant good roots. However, the one cry of 'Namo Buddha' was the good seed which has now ripened and allowed him to leave home and certify to the fruit."

Describing The Substance

The second of the Five-fold Profound Meanings is Describing the Substance. Once you know a person's name, you learn to recognize him on sight. "Is he fat or thin, tall or short?" You don't necessarily have to see his face, but can recognize him by his form. "Oh, it's him."

This sutra is a Mahayana Dharma, spoken without request, and takes the Real Mark as its substance. The Real Mark is no mark. There is no mark, nothing at all, and yet there is nothing which is not marked. Unmarked, it is true emptiness, and with nothing unmarked, it is wonderful existence.

All marks are the Real Mark:

The Real Mark is unmarked
With nothing unmarked.
It is without marks and also without any non-marks.
It is neither without marks nor is it marked by no marks.

While in the midst of marks, one should not hold onto marks, for they are not the Real Mark. True Suchness, the one true Dharma Realm, the Thus Come One's Store Nature, all are different names for the Real Mark.

Clarifying the Principle

Unless you understand the sutra's doctrine and objective, you will not understand its principles. So now we will examine the one by means of the other. It is just like knowing a person's name and then discovering his occupation.

The principles of this sutra are faith, vows, and practice holding the Buddha's name; these are the three prerequisites of the Pure Land dharma-door. One who goes on a journey takes along some food and a little money. One who wishes to go to the Land of Ultimate Bliss needs faith, vows, and the practice of holding the Buddha's name.

Faith

Faith is the first prerequisite, for without it one will not make the vow to be born with Amitabha in the Pure Land of Ultimate Bliss, and thus will not realize the objective of this sutra. You must have faith in yourself, the Land of Ultimate Bliss, cause and effect, and noumena and phenomena.

What does it mean to believe in oneself? It is to believe that you certainly have the qualifications necessary to be born in the Land of Ultimate Bliss. You should not take yourself lightly and say, "I have committed so many offenses, I can't be born there." If you have heavy offense karma, you now have a good opportunity to take it with you to the Land of Ultimate Bliss. Regardless of the offenses you have committed in the past, if you change your mind and reform your conduct, you may be born there, offenses and all.

Taking your karma to the Pure Land refers to past karma, however, not to future karma. Once you have understood the Dharma, offenses should cease. If you continue to offend, you will absolutely not be reborn in the Land of Ultimate Bliss. You may recite the Buddha's name and bow to the Buddha, but you will only be making investments in future Buddhahood. You will not, in this life, be born in the Land of Ultimate Bliss because you clearly understood and yet deliberately violated the rules of the Dharma.

Before taking refuge with the Triple Jewel, doing things which are not in accord with the Dharma may be excusable, but to continue such behavior after taking refuge increases the gravity of one's offenses. Knowing your error, you must truly change your faults and say, "I most certainly can be reborn in the Land of Ultimate Bliss."

Secondly, you must have faith in the Western Land of Ultimate Bliss which is hundreds of thousands of millions of Buddhalands from here. Before he realized Buddhahood, Amitabha Buddha, as the Bhikshu Dharma Treasury, vowed to create a land where living beings who recited his name could be born. There's no need to do anything else; it's easy, simple, and convenient. It doesn't cost a thing, and yet this dharma-door is the highest and most supreme, for if you just recite, "Namo Amitabha Buddha," you will be born in the Land of Ultimate Bliss.

It is also necessary to believe in cause and effect, to believe that in the past you have planted good roots which have caused you to encounter this dharma-door of faith, vows, and holding the Buddha's name. Without good roots, no one can encounter this, or any other dharma-door. But, just as in planting the fields, if a farmer doesn't nourish and irrigate the fields, he won't reap the fruit. So believe that in the past you have planted the causes of Bodhi which in the future will bear the fruit of Bodhi if you just nourish the root.

You may think, "You tell me to believe in cause and effect and to believe that I have good roots, but, frankly, I don't think I do."

How can you tell whether or not you have good roots? People often ask me to tell them whether or not they have good roots, but I tell them to tell me if I have good roots. They say, "I don't know if you do," and I answer them, "then how should I know about you?" But I do have a method to teach you how to find out. You have met the Buddhadharma because you have good roots; without them you would not have had this opportunity.

"Granted, I have met the Buddhadharma," you say, "but is it possible that I have no good roots?"

If you lack them, plant them. If you don't plant them you will never have any! Whether or not you have good roots is no great problem. The question is whether or not you will plant and nourish them by cultivating according to Dharma.

For example, the Buddhadharma teaches you not to drink, but you would risk your life to do it. Drunk, with your head confused and your eyes bleary, your brain feels as if it were going to split open. This is to walk down the road of stupidity.

The Buddhadharma teaches you not to steal, but even if your life were not at stake, you'd steal. One who truly cultivates according to Dharma does not lie, drink, steal, kill, or commit acts of sexual misconduct. Obey the Buddha and refrain from evil. Do not think that minor faults are unimportant, for it's just the minor faults that drag one into the hells or into the paths of hungry ghosts or animals. Believe, then, that you have good roots and that in the future you will reap the fruit of Bodhi.

Finally, one must have faith in the phenomena and the noumena of the *Amitabha Sutra*. The specific phenomena is this: Amitabha Buddha has a great affinity with us and will certainly guide us to Buddhahood. The noumenal principle is this: We know the great affinity exists because without it we would not have met the Pure Land dharma-door. Amitabha Buddha is all living beings and all living beings are Amitabha Buddha. Amitabha Buddha became

Amitabha Buddha by reciting the Buddha's name, and if we recite the Buddha's name, we, too, can become Amitabha Buddha.

We should cultivate according to the phenomenal and the noumenal principles. The *Avatamsaka Sutra* speaks of four Dharma Realms:

1) The Dharma Realm of Unobstructed Phenomena,

2) The Dharma Realm of Unobstructed Noumena,

3) The Dharma Realm of Noumena and Phenomena Unobstructed,

4) The Dharma Realm of All Phenomena Unobstructed.

Considering the four Dharma Realms, and speaking from the standpoint of our self-nature, we and Amitabha Buddha are united in one, and therefore we have the qualifications to realize Buddhahood.

The phenomenon has a mark and a manifestation. It is conditioned. The noumenon is the doctrine underlying any phenomenal event. For example, in principle a tree has the potential to become a house. Before the house is built, it has that noumenal aspect. Once built, the house itself is the phenomenon, which appears because of the noumenon. In principle, we can all realize Buddhahood, but we have not phenomenally done so. If we have faith, vows and hold the name, we will arrive at the phenomena of Buddhahood, just as the tree can be made into a house.

Amitabha Buddha is contained within the hearts of all living beings and living beings are contained within Amitabha's heart. This is the phenomenon and the noumenon. You must believe in the doctrine and energetically practice it by reciting the Buddha's name more and more every day.

When one recites "Namo Amitabha Buddha," in the Western Land of Ultimate Bliss, in one of the pools of the seven jewels filled with the eight waters of merit and virtue, a lotus flower grows. The more one recites, the bigger it grows, but it won't bloom until the end of life, when one's self-nature goes to be reborn in it. If you wish to know whether you will be born in a superior, middle, or inferior grade of lotus, you should ask yourself how often you recite the Buddha's name. The more you recite, the bigger the lotus; the less you recite, the smaller. If you don't recite at all, the lotus withers and dies.

To be reborn in the Land of Ultimate Bliss, you must personally give proof to the result with deep faith, firm vows, and actual practice of recitation. It won't work to think, "I'll sleep-in today and cultivate tomorrow." If, however, you hold fast to the name and cultivate vigorously, success is certain.

Vows

Having discussed faith, we will now discuss vows. What is a vow? What you wish[16], the tendency of your thoughts, is a vow. In Buddhism there are four great vows:

> *I vow to save the limitless living beings.*
> *I vow to cut off the inexhaustible afflictions.*
> *I vow to study the immeasurable dharma-doors.*
> *I vow to realize the supreme Buddha Way.*

All Buddhas and Bodhisattvas of the past, present, and future practiced the Bodhisattva conduct and attained Buddhahood by relying on these four great vows.

You may make the four great vows according to the Four Holy Truths.

> *According to the truth of suffering,*
> *I vow to save the limitless living beings.*
> *According to the truth of origination,*
> *I vow to cut off the inexhaustible afflictions.*
> *According to the truth of the Way,*
> *I vow to study the immeasurable dharma-doors.*

---

16. The Chinese word for vow, *yuan* 愿, also means "to wish" or "to want."

According to the truth of extinction,
I vow to realize the supreme Buddha Way.

The four great vows come from an awareness of the suffering of living beings. For purposes of clarification, suffering is divided into groups of the three, eight, and limitless sufferings.

According to the truth of origination, I vow to cut off the inexhaustible afflictions:

The three sufferings are:

1) Suffering within suffering. This is the poverty and misery of all living beings.

2) The suffering of decay. Living beings may enjoy wealth and honor, but it eventually goes bad.

3) The suffering of process. Even without the sufferings of poverty and decay, the bitterness of the life-process from birth, to the prime of life, to old age and then to death is still suffering. The shift and change of each passing thought is called the suffering of process.

The eight sufferings are:

1) The suffering of birth.

2) The suffering of old age.

3) The suffering of sickness.

4) The suffering of death.

It was because Shakyamuni Buddha met with these four sufferings that he decided to leave the home-life and cultivate the Way.

5) The suffering of separation from what you love.

6) The suffering of being joined with what you hate.

If people are not apart from loved ones, they are involved with enemies. If you don't like someone, you'll find someone just like him wherever you go.

7) The suffering of not realizing aspirations.

You worry about getting something and once you have it you worry about losing it. This suffering is nothing compared to the next:

8) The suffering of the raging blaze of the five skandhas: form, feelings, perceptions, impulses, and consciousness. The five skandhas are like a raging fire. They are a constant shadow which we cannot escape.

According to the truth of suffering, I vow to save the limitless living beings:

Why are there limitless sufferings besides these eight?

In the past lives we planted the seeds of suffering as if they were old friends with which we were loathe to part. Having established causes and conditions for suffering in the past, in the present we reap a bitter fruit.

> *From causes made in lives gone by*
> *comes your present life;*
> *Results you'll get in lives to come*
> *arise from this life's deeds.*
>
> *Plant good causes, reap good results;*
> *Plant bad causes, reap bad results.*

You fear the results. "Oh, I'm suffering too bitterly," you say, but you suffer because previously you planted the causes of suffering.

Living beings fear the results, not the causes from which they come, but Bodhisattvas fear the causes, not the results. Bodhisattvas are extremely careful not to plant the causes of suffering and so they do not reap the harvest of suffering. They endure their present suffering gladly. So Bodhisattvas, too, must sometimes suffer, but they do so willingly, knowing that

Enduring suffering ends suffering;
Enjoying blessings destroys blessings.

Living beings, on the other hand, are not afraid to plant the causes of suffering. "Good causes, bad causes, it doesn't matter," they say, "I'll do it anyway. It's not important." But when the results come, "Oh! I can't stand it," they moan. "How could this happen to me? Such bitterness!"

If you fear suffering you should not plant the causes of suffering, for if you do, you will certainly reap its bitter fruit.

Born in the Land of Ultimate Bliss, one endures no suffering but enjoys every bliss. None of the three sufferings, eight sufferings, or the limitless sufferings are found there at all. The people are pure and free of greed, hatred, and stupidity. Without the three poisons there are no evil paths of rebirth because the evil paths are but manifestations of the poisons.

The Buddha saves living beings, but in reality there is not a single living being that he saves. He resolves to lead everyone to understand the Buddhadharma in order to leave suffering, attain bliss, and wake up. But when you take beings across, do not become attached to the mark of taking beings across.

Take living beings across, but be apart from marks.
Leave marks, yet take beings across.

Do not attach to some mark or sign of what you do and say, "Let's see, I've saved three, four... six, seven... at least ten living beings!" If you keep count, you've still got attachments.

Save, yet do not save;
Do not save, yet save:
This is true crossing over.

You must save the living beings within your own self-nature as well as those outside. There are eighty-four thousand living beings in your self-nature. Teach them to cultivate, realize Buddhahood, and enter Nirvana.

If you decide to save living beings, you will encounter afflictions; if you don't save them, you will also have afflictions. Either way you will have afflictions because there are eighty-four thousand kinds of affliction.

There are three delusions:

1) Delusions of views and thought.
2) Delusions like dust and sand.
3) Delusions of ignorance.

Living beings have all three types of delusions. Those of the Small Vehicle have cut off the delusions of views and thought, but retain the delusions like dust and sand and the delusions of ignorance. Bodhisattvas have cut off both the delusions of views and thought and the delusions like dust and sand, but they still have delusions of ignorance. Even Bodhisattvas at the stage of Equal Enlightenment who are just about to realize Buddhahood, still have one particle of "production-mark" ignorance as fine as a hair which they have not yet destroyed. This particle once destroyed, they attain the Wonderful Enlightenment of Buddhahood.

The delusion of views refers to greed and love for externals. Because external objects are not viewed as empty, they are recognized as real. Clothing, food, and sleep seem very real. "It's true," you say, "I'm all alone. I have no friends or relatives." This confused state is the delusion of views. Not understanding what you see, you are greedy for comfort and "good" things. "I love this and I love that," you say, and your endless love keeps you dissatisfied and greedy for externals. This is the delusion of views.

The delusion of thought consists in being confused about principles and giving rise to discrimination. "I don't know what's going on here," someone says. "Is the Dharma Master right? If I do what he says, what's in it for me?" You constantly calculate about personal advantage, and, if there's nothing in it for you, you don't want to do it. You can't see more than three inches beyond your face. Anything four inches away you cannot see. Thought delusions are unclear, muddled thoughts, taking what is wrong as right, and what is right as wrong.

I just said that people with view delusions think clothing, food, and sleep are real. Someone may ask if they are false, and, if so, then what is true? These things are all necessities, but if you attach no importance to them, you are relaxed and free. Whenever there is attachment, there is pain. If you take it all as unreal, there will be no greed or love, and you will see that your former greed and love were nothing but confused actions in a dream. You should think of them in this way; put everything down; let it all go. If you can't put it down, you're attached, and nothing goes right.

There are eighty-eight parts to the delusion of views and eighty-one parts to the delusion of thought. When the delusion of views is destroyed, you certify to the first fruit of Arhatship. If not, there is no certification.

Do you have greed and love for externals? Are you greedy for "good" things and repulsed by the bad?

"Absolutely not," you say.

How do you know you are not? If you really didn't love the good and hate the bad you wouldn't know it. If you say, "I know for certain that I have no greed or love," then your greed and love is greater than anyone else's. Why? Because you know that you have none. If you really had none you wouldn't know that you didn't. If you say that you have no self, how do you know that you have no self? Knowing that you have no self, you still have your "self." If you say that you have no greed or love, you still have a self and you haven't cut off the eighty-eight parts of the delusion of views and you haven't certified to the first fruit of Arhatship. It is not simply a matter of saying it and making it so. You must truly attain this state.

The delusion of views contains the five quick servants and the delusions of thought contain the five dull servants. The five dull servants are greed, hatred, stupidity, pride and doubt. The five quick servants are said to be "quick" because they arrive very fast. The five dull servants arrive more slowly.

The Five Quick Servants are:

1) The view of a body. Because one is attached, one thinks, "This is my body, and I'm so thin! I'm not eating right, I'm not properly dressed, and I don't have a decent place to live. How can I take care of my body?" Attached to the body and holding a view of a body, one schemes for it all day long.

2) The view of extremes. To become attached to either of the two extreme views of permanence or annihilation is to indulge in this view. Attached to annihilation, one says, "People die, and that is that. Everything returns to emptiness."

Attached to permanence, one says, "Next life I'll be a person again. People are always people and dogs are always dogs. Cats are always cats, horses are always horses, trees are always trees, grass is always grass. People can't become cats and cats can't turn into people. People can't turn into animals or ghosts. This is the fixed, eternal, unchanging principle: permanence." Annihilation and permanence are extreme views; they are not the Middle Way.

3) Deviant views. Those with deviant views say that when one does good there is no good retribution and when one does evil there is no evil retribution. They deny cause and effect and do not believe that by doing good deeds one obtains blessings and by doing evil deeds one incurs disaster.

4) The views of restrictive morality. This is to take a non-existent cause for a true cause; for example, teaching others to imitate the conduct of dogs and cats, or to imitate cows and eat grass instead of food. Having seen a dog or cat reborn in the heavens one may want to imitate a dog or cat and thereby hold deviant knowledge and views.

Sometimes people who have left the home-life are attached to keeping the precepts. "I hold the precepts," they brag. "I am a precept-holder and these are the precepts I hold." Because there is a "holder" and "that which is held" they do not understand that the basic substance of morality is empty. They shouldn't have attachments, but they do, and this turns into this servant.

5) The view of grasping at views. Here, a non-existent effect is taken to be a true effect. The non-ultimate is considered to be ultimate. The four Dhyanas or the four stations of emptiness are mistaken for Nirvana.

a) In the first Dhyana, the pulse stops.

b) In the second Dyana, the breath stops. One sits without breathing, but if one thinks, "I'm not breathing," then the breath starts up again.

c) In the third Dhyana there is no thought. In the first and second, although there is neither pulse nor breath, thinking continues. In the third, there isn't even any thought.

d) In the fourth Dhyana, there isn't any fine thought, only consciousness. In the third Dhyana, although there is no coarse thought, fine thought remains. In the fourth, fine thought is also cut off.

These are just states; they are not the ultimate goal of cultivation, which is certification to the fruit. Even the four stations of emptiness:

1) The station of infinite space,

2) The station of infinite consciousness,

3) The station of nothing whatever, and

4) The station of neither perception nor non-perception, are not certification to the fruit. They are simply levels of samadhi.

Those who hold the view of grasping at views think that the above-mentioned states are Nirvana, like the untutored Bhikshu who mistook the fourth Dhyana heaven for the fourth fruit of Arhatship. When the merit which had enabled him to dwell there was used up and he started to fall, he slandered the Dharma, and because of this he fell into hell.

The five quick servants are the delusion of views and are called "quick" because they arrive quickly.

Referring to the delusion of thought and arriving more slowly are the Five Dull Servants:

1) Greed.
2) Hatred.
3) Stupidity.
4) Pride.
5) Doubt.

Afflictions come from ignorance. When the delusions of ignorance arise, delusions like dust and sand follow. The delusions like dust and sand are called the delusions of "I don't know" because there is no genuine knowledge. The delusions of views and thought are called the delusions of "I don't see."

Ignorance turns into the first of the five dull servants, greed. When you want something, greed arises, and with it come all the various afflictions. The afflictions turn into hatred, and you argue on your own behalf, never seeing the other person's side. You only know yourself and are unaware that other people exist, except in attempting to ruin them. In this way, reckless and unreasonable, you become stupid, unable to tell black from white, right from wrong.

Stupid people are arrogant, and no matter what you say they doubt it. They doubt the truth and doubt the false even more. All these doubts are the delusions of thought.

The three categories of delusions, those of views and thought, dust and sand, and ignorance, all change into affliction. Afflictions are inexhaustible and endless. Observing this, cultivators vow: *According to the truth of origination, I vow to cut off the inexhaustible afflictions.*

According to the truth of the Way, I vow to study the immeasurable dharma doors:

To cultivate the Way, you must understand all of the limitless and unbounded dharma-doors, which are the methods of cultivation. Unless you understand them, you cannot cultivate. Relying on the third Holy Truth, the Way, vow to study them.

What is the origin of the dharma-doors?

> *The Buddhas spoke all dharmas*
> *for the minds of men.*
> *If there were no minds,*
> *What use would dharmas be?*

All dharmas come from the minds of living beings, and each mind is unique. Since no two minds are alike, all dharma-doors differ. Generally speaking, however, there are three classes of dharmas:

1) Buddhadharma
2) Mind-dharma
3) Dharma of living beings.

Within the three classes arise the Four Holy Truths, the Six Perfections, the Twelve Causes and Conditions, and the Thirty-Seven Limbs of Enlightenment. So many dharma-doors!

Take, for example, my explanations of the sutras. When I finish explaining one sutra, I begin another, and no sooner have I finished that one, than I start yet another. Isn't this measureless? What we now study is like a drop of water in the sea. We certainly haven't got the entire ocean. Vow to master the immeasurable dharma-doors.

"What are the advantages of studying the Buddhadharma?" you ask. "It's a lot of trouble, you know."

We study the Buddhadharma because we want to realize Buddhahood.

"But isn't wanting to realize Buddhahood just another false thought?"

No, it's not a false thought. Buddhahood was our position to begin with; it is our origin. Consequently, everyone can realize Buddhahood, and we should hurry up and do just that.

"But how?"

According to the truth of extinction, I vow to realize the supreme Buddha Way:

The truth of extinction is the attainment of Nirvana, a realization which carries one beyond production and extinction. If this attainment is your wish, resolve to cultivate the supreme Buddha Way. Don't be skeptical and ask, "Can I really become a Buddha?" Even if you have doubts, you can become a Buddha; it will take a little longer, that's all. Without doubts you can do it right away. All living beings have the Buddha nature and all can realize Buddhahood. But this does not mean that all beings *are* Buddhas. To arrive at Buddhahood you must cultivate, for without cultivation living beings are just living beings, not Buddhas. In principle, everyone can become a Buddha, but unless you cultivate according to Dharma and rid yourself of greed, hatred, stupidity, pride, and doubt, you won't become a Buddha very fast. This completes the discussion of the four vast vows.

If you wish to accomplish something, you should first make a vow. Then act upon it. In this way you will naturally attain your aim. This principle is illustrated by the following story:

Once, Shakyamuni Buddha and his disciple Mahamaudgalyayana went with a large gathering of followers to another county to convert living beings. When the citizens saw the Buddha they shut their doors and ignored him. When they saw Maudgalyayana, however, they ran to greet him, and everyone, from the King and ministers to the citizens, all bowed and competed to make offerings to him. The Buddha's disciples thought this most unfair. "World Honored One," they said, "your virtuous conduct is so lofty; why is it they do not make offerings to you, but instead compete to make offerings to Maudgalyayana?"

"This is because of past affinities," said the Buddha. "I will tell you...

"Limitless aeons ago, Maudgalyayana and I were fellow countrymen. He gathered firewood in the mountains and I lived in a hut below. A swarm of bees was bothering me and I decided to smoke them out. But Maudgalyayana refused to help even though they stung him until his hands were swollen and painful. Instead, he made a vow, 'It must be miserable to be a bee,' he thought. 'I vow that when I attain the Way I will take these asura-like bees across first thing!'

"Many lifetimes later the bees were reborn as the citizens of this country. The queen bee became the King, the drones became the ministers, and the workers became the citizens. Because I didn't like the bees, I now have no affinity with these people and therefore no one makes offerings to me. But, because of his vows, all the citizens revere Maudgalyayana."

Considering this, we should certainly make vows to establish affinities in order to benefit living creatures.

Practice: Holding The Name

> *When the water-clearing pearl*
> *is tossed in muddy water,*
> *The muddy water becomes clear.*

> *When the Buddha's name*
> *enters a confused mind,*
> *The confused mind attains to the Buddha.*

This sutra takes faith, vows, and holding the name as its doctrine. Having discussed faith and vows, we shall now discuss holding the name.

Reciting the Buddha's name is like throwing a pearl into muddy water so that the muddy water becomes clear. This clear-water pearl can purify even the filthiest water. Recitation of the Buddha's name is like this pearl.

Who can count the false thoughts which fill our minds and succeed one another endlessly like waves on the sea? When the Buddha's name enters a confused mind, the confused mind becomes the Buddha. Recite the name once and there is one Buddha in your mind; recite it ten times and there are ten Buddhas, recite it a hundred times and there are a hundred Buddhas. The more you recite, the more Buddhas there are.

Say, "Namo Amitabha Buddha," there's a Buddha-thought in your mind. When you are mindful of the Buddha, the Buddha is mindful of you. It's like communication by radio or radar. You recite here, and it's received there. But if you don't recite, nothing is received; so you must hold and recite the name.

In the Dharma-ending age, recitation of the Buddha's name is a most important dharma-door. Don't take it lightly. Every time Dhyana Master Yong Ming Shou, the Sixth Patriarch of the Pure Land School, recited the Buddha's name, a transformation Buddha came out of his mouth. Those with the Five Eyes and Six Spiritual Penetrations could see it. When you recite the Buddha's name, you emit a light which frightens all weird creatures and strange ghosts away. They run far, far away and leave you alone. So the merit and virtue of holding the Buddha's name is inconceivable.

Holding and reciting the Buddha's name, you should, as it says in the *Doctrine of the Mean*, "grasp it tightly in your fist." Do not let it go. Thought after thought, recite the name. There are four methods of reciting.

1) Contemplating and thinking Buddha-recitation.

2) Contemplating an image Buddha-recitation.

3) Real Mark Buddha-recitation.

4) Holding the name Buddha-recitation.

The first, contemplating and thinking Buddha recitation, consists of the contemplation of Amitabha Buddha:

Amitabha Buddha's body is of golden hue,
His fine marks radiant beyond compare.
His white light is as high as five Mount Sumerus,
His purple eyes as clear and vast as four great seas.

Countless transformation Buddhas appear within the light,
With transformation Bodhisattvas, also limitless.
His forty-eight vows take living beings across;
In nine grades of lotuses they ascend to the other shore.

Amitabha Buddha's appearance is the result of the perfection of his merit and virtue. He has all of the 32 marks and the 80 minor characteristics of a Buddha and his bright light is incomparable. Between his eyebrows there are fine white beams of light as big as five Mount Sumerus, and his eyes are as large as four great seas. How big do you think his body is?

There are nine grades of lotuses:

1) Superior superior
2) Superior middle
3) Superior inferior
4) Middle superior
5) Middle middle
6) Middle inferior
7) Inferior superior
8) Inferior middle
9) Inferior inferior

Each of the nine grades also has nine ranks, making 81 in all. Living beings in all of these grades are led to the other shore – Nirvana.

The second kind of Buddha-recitation, contemplating the image, consists of making offerings to an image of Amitabha

Buddha and reciting his name while contemplating it. Contemplate, and in time you will have success.

When you achieve the third, Real Mark recitation, even if you try, you cannot stop reciting the Buddha's name. The recitation flows like water and lives within you. This is the state of the Buddha-recitation samadhi: reciting and yet not reciting, not reciting and yet reciting.

The fourth kind of Buddha-recitation is that of holding the name. Both moving and still, one recites, "Namo Amitabha Buddha." Recitation must be clear and distinct and the three karmas of body, mouth, and mind must be pure. The mouth is free from the four evil karmas of

1) abusive language,
2) profanity,
3) lying, and
4) gossip,

and the body is without the three evil karmas of

5) killing,
6) stealing, or
7) sexual misconduct.

The mind has no

8) greed,
9) hatred, or
10) stupidity.

When one is free of the ten evil deeds, then the karma of body, mouth, and mind is pure. In this way, one thought pure is one thought of the Buddha; when every thought is pure, every thought is of the Buddha.

The pure heart is like the moon in the water;
The mind in samadhi is like the cloudless sky.

If you can recite so completely that you enter the Buddha-recitation samadhi, then hearing the wind, it's "Namo Amitabha Buddha," and hearing the rain, it's "Namo Amitabha Buddha." Every sound you hear recites the Buddha's name.

The water flows,
The wind blows,
Proclaiming the Mahayana...

The Chinese poet Su Dong Po said,

Of the colors of the mountain,
None are not his vast, long tongue.
Of the sounds of the streams,
All are the clear, pure sound.

All the mountain's colors are the Buddha's long tongue proclaiming the wonderful Dharma. This is the attainment of the Buddha-recitation samadhi.

So I wrote this verse:

If you recite the Buddha's name,
*   reciting without cease,*
The mouth recite "Amita"
*   and makes things of a piece.*
Scattered thoughts do not arise,
*   samadhi you attain.*
For rebirth in the Pure Land,
*   your hope is not in vain.*

If all day you detest
*   the suffering Saha's pain,*
Make rebirth in Ultimate Bliss
*   your mind's essential aim.*
Cut off the red dust
*   thoughts within your mind.*

Put down impure reflections,
and pure thoughts you will find.

Recite the Buddha's name from morning to night and your confused thoughts will not arise. You will naturally attain the Buddha-recitation samadhi and be reborn in the Land of Ultimate Bliss, according to your will. You know that the Saha world is full of pain and suffering; so cut off worldly pleasures and have no thoughts of sexual desire, craving, or struggling for fame and profit. Put down all worldly concerns and view them as false. Seek rebirth, ultimate bliss; this thought of rebirth is extremely important.

The verse clearly explains the principles of reciting the Buddha's name. Holding and reciting the name is like picking up something in your hand and never letting it go. Recite "Namo Amitabha Buddha" every day and chase out your scattered thoughts.

This dharma-door fights poison with poison. False thinking is like poison, and unless you counter it with poison, you will never cure it. Reciting the Buddha's name is fighting false thinking with false thinking. It is like sending out an army to defeat an army, to fight a battle to end all battles. If you have a good defense, other countries won't attack. Constant recitation drives out false thinking so that you may attain the Buddha-recitation samadhi.

The third of the Five-fold Profound Meanings, then, is to take Faith, Vows, and Holding the Name as the doctrine.

Discussing the Function

The fourth of the Five-fold Profound Meanings is to determine the sutra's power and use. Its power is that of "non-retreat" and its use is rebirth. Reborn in the Land of Ultimate Bliss, you attain to the stage of no retreat. Cultivators of other dharma-doors are somewhat insecure; no one insures them. They may recite mantras or sutras for several years and then retreat with a feeling of no accomplishment or gain. If not in this life, they may retreat in the next. Perhaps they are vigorous now, but later they take a rest. To say nothing of common people, even Arhats have the "confusion of dwelling in the womb" and forget their spiritual penetrations. Bodhisattvas have the confusion called "splitting the *yin*," which means the same thing. If they meet a good knowing advisor who teaches them to cultivate, they can wake up. Otherwise, life after life, they retreat and find it very hard to bring forth the Bodhi-heart again. It is easy to regress.

Born in the Land of Ultimate Bliss, there is no back-sliding, just vigorous progress. One attains the four kinds of Non-retreat:

1) Non-retreating position. Born in the Land of Ultimate Bliss, you attain the Buddha-position. Born by transformation from a lotus, when the flower blooms, you see the Buddha, hear the Dharma, awaken to the unproduced dharma-patience, and never fall again.

2) Non-retreating conduct. Most people cultivate vigorously for one life, but in the next, they are lazy. In the Land of Ultimate

Bliss there is none of the suffering of the three evil paths. The Kalavinka birds and two-headed birds all help Amitabha Buddha speak about the Dharma. Reborn there, one will no longer be lazy in conduct but will only go forward with courage and vigor.

3) Non-retreating thought. In the Saha world we cultivate vigorously, but after a time we feel it's too bitter, too restrictive, too uncomfortable, and so we are no longer vigorous. Lazy thoughts arise and although we have not yet retreated in conduct, we have in thought. Several decades pass quickly and thoughts of retreat greatly out-number those of vigor. It's difficult not to regress.

In the Land of Ultimate Bliss, one hears the Dharma spoken all day and all night long. One has no thoughts of retreat from the Bodhi-mind. All thoughts are irreversible.

4) Ultimate Non-retreat. Transformationally born from a lotus, you will never, under any circumstances, retreat again either to the level of a common person or to the Small Vehicle or Bodhisattva level. Born in the Land of Ultimate Bliss you obtain these four kinds of Non-retreat.

Determining the Teaching Mark

The *Tripitaka* is divided into three parts: *Sutras*, which deal with samadhi, *Sastras*, which deal with wisdom, and *Vinaya*, which deal with morality. This text belongs to the sutra division, and as such it is permanent and unchanging, two characteristics of sutras. When all other Buddhadharmas have become extinct, this sutra will remain in the world an additional hundred years and save limitless living beings. For this reason, it differs from other sutras.

Of the three vehicles, Sravakas, Conditionally Enlightened Ones, and Bodhisattvas, this sutra belongs to the Bodhisattva Vehicle. It takes across Bodhisattvas suited to the Great Vehicle.

Knowing the sutra's title classification and its Five-fold Profound Meanings, we now have a general understanding of the *Buddha Speaks of Amitabha Sutra*.

PART II

THE TRANSLATOR

Sutra:

Translated by Tripitaka Master Kumarajiva of Yao Qin.

Commentary:

Yao Qin is the name of the reign period of emperor Yao Xing. It is not the same period as that of Qin Shi Huang called the Ying Qing, or that of Fu Jian, which is called Fu Qin.

Before the time of Emperor Yao Xing, and during the time of Fu Jian, a man named Qin Tian Jian said to Fu Jian, "Now one of great wisdom should come to China to aid our government."

Fu Jian said, "It is probably Kumarajiva, for he is honored and respected in India for his wisdom."

Kumarajiva.

Kumarajiva's father, Kumarayana, was the son of a prime minister. He should have succeeded his father, but instead he left his home and went everywhere looking for a teacher. Although he hadn't left the home-life in the formal sense by taking the complete precepts, he still cultivated the Way, and in his travels went to the country of Kucha in central Asia. The King of Kucha had a little sister, and when she saw Kumarayana she said to the King, "I really love this man." The King gave his sister in marriage to Kumarayana and she soon became pregnant.

When Kumarajiva was still in his mother's womb, it was much like the situation with Shariputra and his mother. Kumarajiva's mother could defeat everyone in debate. At that time an Arhat said, "The child in this woman's womb is certainly one of great wisdom."

When Kumarajiva was seven years old, his mother took him to a temple to worship the Buddha. Kumarajiva picked up a large bronze incense urn and effortlessly lifted it over his head. Then he thought, "Hey, I'm just a child. How can I lift this heavy urn?" With this one thought, the urn crashed to the ground. From this he realized the meaning of the doctrine, "Everything is made from the mind alone," and he and his mother left the home-life.

Kumarajiva's mother had difficulty leaving the home-life. Although Kumarajiva's father had previously cultivated the Way, he was now too much in love with his wife to permit her to leave home. Thereupon, she went on a strict fast. "Unless you allow me to leave home," she said, "I won't eat or drink. I'll starve myself."

"Then don't eat or drink, if that's what you want," said her husband, "but I'll never let you leave home."

For six days she didn't eat or drink, not even fruit juice, and she became extremely weak. Finally, Kumarayana said, "This is too dangerous. You're going to starve to death. You may leave home, but please eat something."

"First call in a Dharma Master to cut off my hair," she said, "and then I'll eat." A Dharma Master came and shaved her head, and then she ate. Shortly after leaving home, she certified to the first fruit of Arhatship.

Soon after that, Kumarajiva, her son, also left the home-life. Everyday he read and recited many sutras, and once he read them, he never forgot them. He was not like some of you who have recited the Shurangama Mantra for several months, but still need the book. Because of his faultless memory he defeated all non-Buddhist philosophers in India and became very well known.

His reputation spread to China, and when Fu Jian heard of him he sent the great General Lu Guang and seventy thousand troops to Kucha to capture Kumarajiva and bring him back to China. Kumarajiva said to the King of Kucha, "China is sending troops, but do not oppose them. They don't wish to take the country. They have another purpose and you should grant them their request."

The King's uncle wouldn't listen to Kumarajiva and he went to war with the general from China, Lu Guang. As a result, the King of Kucha was put to death, the country defeated, and Kumarajiva captured.

On the way back to China, General Lu Guang one day prepared to camp in a low valley. Kumarajiva, who had spiritual powers, knew a rain was coming which would flood the valley. He told the General, "Don't camp here tonight. This place is dangerous."

But Lu Guang had no faith in Kumarajiva. "You're a monk," he said. "What do you know about military affairs?" That night there was a deluge and many men and horses were drowned. General Lu Guang then knew that Kumarajiva was truly inconceivable.

They proceeded until they heard that there had been a change in the Chinese government. Emperor Fu Jian had been deposed, and Yao Chang had seized the throne. General Lu Guang maintained his neutrality, and did not return to China. Yao Chang was Emperor for several years, and when he died, his nephew Yao Xing took the throne. It was Yao Xing who dispatched a party to invite Kumarajiva to China to translate sutras. A gathering of over eight-hundred Bhikshus assembled to assist him in this work.

We have proof that Kumarajiva's translations are extremely accurate. When he was about to complete the stillness, that is, die, he said, "I have translated numerous sutras during my life-time, and I personally don't know if my translations are correct. If they are, when I am cremated my tongue will not burn; but if there are mistakes, it will." When he died, his body was burned, but his tongue remained intact.

The Tang dynasty Vinaya Master Dao Xuan once asked the god Lu Xuan Chang, "Why does everyone prefer to read and study Kumarajiva's translations?" The god replied, "Kumarajiva has been the Translation Master for the past seven Buddhas and so his translations are accurate."

The *Tripitaka* is the collection of Buddhist scriptures. It is divided into three parts: *sutras*, which deal with samadhi, *sastras*, which deal with wisdom, and the *vinaya*, which is the study of moral precepts.

A Dharma Master 1) takes the Dharma as his master and 2) gives the Dharma to others. Some Dharma Masters chant sutras, some maintain them in their minds and practice them with their bodies, some write them out, and some explain them to others.

The Dharma Master spoken of here is Kumarajiva. This Sanskrit name means "youth of long life." One could say, "Young Kumarajiva will certainly live to a great age." One could also say, "He is young in years, but mature in wisdom, eloquence, and virtue. He has the wisdom of an old, old man, and so he is called "Youth of Long Life.""[17]

It was Kumarajiva, the youth with the virtuous conduct of an elder, who translated the *Buddha Speaks of Amitabha Sutra* from Sanskrit into Chinese.

---

17. *tong shou* 童壽

PART III

THE PREFACE

All sutras may be divided into three parts:

1) the Preface,
2) the Principle Proper, and
3) the Transmission.

The Preface discusses the sutra's general meaning, the Principle Proper discusses its doctrines, and the Transmission instructs us to transmit the sutra, to propagate it and make it flow, like water, everywhere. The Preface is like a person's head, and the Principle Proper is like his body. Just as our organs are very clearly arranged within our bodies, so are the doctrines clearly set forth within the sutras.

The Preface may also be called the "Afterword." "Isn't that a contradiction," you ask. It is not a contradiction because it wasn't spoken by Shakyamuni Buddha himself, but was added later when Ananda and Mahakasyapa edited the sutras. It may also be called the "Arising of Dharma" Preface because it sets forth the reasons the sutra was spoken. It is also called the "Certification of Faith" Preface because it proves that the sutra can be believed.

In the Preface, Six Requirements are fulfilled. They are

1) faith,
2) hearer,
3) time,
4) host,
5) place, and
6) audience.

Sutra:

Thus I have heard. At one time the Buddha dwelt at Sravasti, in the Jeta Grove, in the Garden of the Benefactor of Orphans and the Solitary, together with a gathering of great Bhikshus, twelve hundred fifty in all, all great Arhats whom the assembly knew and recognized:

Commentary:

Thus fulfills the requirement of faith. **I have heard** fulfills the requirement of the hearer. **At one time** fulfills the requirement of time and the **Buddha** is the host. **Sravasti, in the Garden of the Benefactor of Orphans and the Solitary** fulfills the requirement of place, the **gathering of great Bhikshus** fulfills the audience requirement. Because all six requirements are fulfilled, we know that the sutra can be believed.

Thus I have heard.

What does **Thus** mean? **Thus** fills the requirement of faith. You can have faith in Dharma which is **Thus**, not in dharma which is not **Thus**. **Thus** designates the text as orthodox Buddhadharma.

Thus means "it is Thus."

Thus is stillness: *it is* denotes movement.

If it is *Thus*, it is; if it is not *Thus*, it is not.

Whatever is not non-existent, exists; whatever is without error is correct.

Thus means "still and unmoving."

Thus is true emptiness; *it is* is wonderful existence.

Wonderful existence is not apart from true emptiness.

True emptiness is not apart from wonderful existence.

Emptiness and existence are non-dual:

Both empty and existing, neither empty nor existing.

This Dharma can be believed.

The four words **Thus I have heard** begin all Buddhist sutras. It is **Thus**; if it were not **Thus** it would not be correct. This is the doctrine, and Dharma which is **Thus** can be believed.

I have heard.

Ananda says that he himself personally heard this teaching. But, having given proof to the fruit of Arhatship, basically Ananda has no ego. How can he say, "I have heard?" This is the "self of no-self." Ananda says, "I have heard" in order to be comprehensible to ordinary people, who have a "self."

Heard fills the accomplishment of the hearer. Why does one have faith? Because one has heard. If one hadn't heard, how could one have faith?

Ananda's Four Questions

The use of **Thus I have heard** comes from instructions given to Ananda by the Buddha just before the Buddha entered Nirvana:

One day Shakyamuni Buddha announced, "Tonight, in the middle of the night, I am going to enter Nirvana!" When Ananda heard this he was so distraught that he cried like a baby for its mother and called, "Buddha, Buddha, please don't enter Nirvana! Please don't cast us all aside!" He cried and pleaded until his brain got addled, probably because he thought that this was what he should be doing.

Just then a blind man came by, one unlike other blind men. His ordinary eyes were blind, but his Heavenly Eye was open. Because he was blind, he wasn't burdened with a lot of false thinking, and his mind was very clear. "Venerable One," he said, addressing Ananda, "Why are you crying?"

"The Buddha is about to enter Nirvana," Ananda replied. "How can I hold back my tears?"

The eyeless elder replied, "How can you do your work if you cry? After the Buddha enters Nirvana, we will have to establish many things. There is work to be done and questions to be asked."

"What questions?" said Ananda. "The Buddha is going to Nirvana. What is there left to do? What could be more important than the Buddha's Nirvana?"

The blind man, whose name was Aniruddha, and who was foremost in the capacity of the Heavenly Eye, said, "There are four extremely important matters which must be settled."

"What are they?" asked Ananda.

"Compiling the sutras is one," he said. "With what words should we begin each sutra?"

"True!" said Ananda. "That is important. It's a good thing you brought it up. I never would have thought of it myself. All I can think of is the Buddha going to Nirvana. What is the second question I should ask?"

The Venerable Aniruddha said, "We have taken the Buddha as our teacher, but when he goes to Nirvana, who will be our teacher? Should we look for another teacher?"

"Right, right!" said Ananda. "We should find another good teacher. You're quite right. What is the third?"

Aniruddha said, "Now we live with the Buddha, but when he goes to Nirvana, where will we live?"

"That is very important," said Ananda. "Without a place to live, how can we cultivate the Way? Should we find someplace else to live? These three matters are extremely important. What is the fourth?"

Aniruddha said, "The Buddha can discipline evil-natured Bhikshus, but after he goes to Nirvana, how shall we take care of them?"

Now, an evil-natured Bhikshu does nothing but disturb other people. If you meditate, he walks around, "Clomp! Clomp!" making a lot of noise so that no one can enter samadhi. When people are walking, he sits to meditate. "Look at me!" he says. "I sit much better than all of you," and pretends to have entered samadhi. When people are bowing to the Buddha, the evil-natured Bhikshu likes to recite sutras, and when people are reciting sutras, he likes to bow to the Buddha. In general, he's got to have a special style – "the evil-natured-Bhikshu style" – and he does not follow the rules.

If everyone goes one way, he goes the opposite way. He has no consideration for anyone else, but expects everyone to notice him. "He's terrific," everyone says. "He really cultivates." He insists on being special so that others will notice him and say that he is the best. Fiercely competitive, he must be the strongest, outstanding among the best. He stands like an asura with his hands on his hips as if to say, "See what a great hero I am?" He has to be different and outdo everyone else.

When the Buddha was in the world, he could control such evil natured Bhikshus, and they obeyed his instructions. But after he entered Nirvana who would supervise them? And who could control the evil-natured laymen who say, "Look at me. I'm more dedicated than all you other laymen." Actually, it's just because of him and his special style that no one else is dedicated. Aniruddha said, "When the Buddha goes to Nirvana, what are we going to do with the evil-natured Bhikshus and evil-natured laymen?"

"These are important questions," said Ananda. "I'll go ask right away." He wiped his eyes, blew his nose, and ran off to the Buddha. "Buddha, Great Master," he said, "I have four questions which I would like to ask you before you go to Nirvana. World Honored One, won't you be compassionate and answer them?"

"All right," said the Buddha.

"Buddha," said Ananda, "you have spoken many sutras. When we compile and edit them, with what words should they begin?"

The Buddha said, "All sutras spoken by the Buddhas of the past, present, and future begin with the words, 'Thus I have heard,' which means, 'The Dharma which is Thus can be believed. I personally heard it.'"

Ananda said, "Secondly, you are our Master, but when you enter Nirvana, who will be our teacher? Please instruct us. Should it be Mahakasyapa?"

The Buddha said, "No. When I go to Nirvana, take the *Pratimoksa*, the precepts, as your teacher. To accord with the

Buddha's instructions, those who leave home must first receive the precepts."

Then Ananda said, "We have always lived with you, Buddha, but when you enter Nirvana, where are we going to live?"

Shakyamuni Buddha said, "When I go to Nirvana, all Bhikshus, Bhikshunis, Upasakas, and Upasikas should dwell in the Four Applications of Mindfulness: Mindfulness with regard to the body, feelings, thoughts, and dharmas.

1) Contemplate the body as impure. If you know that the body is impure, you won't love it, and without love there will be no attachment. Being without attachment is freedom. So first of all, regard the body as impure.

2) Contemplate feelings as suffering. Feelings are all a kind of suffering, whether they are pleasant or unpleasant, for pleasant feelings are the cause of unpleasant feelings.

3) Contemplate thought as impermanent. Thoughts shift and flow and are not permanent.

4) Contemplate dharmas as devoid of self."

Ananda further asked, "How should we treat evil-natured Bhikshus?"

The Buddha said, "That is no problem at all. Simply be silent and they will go away. Fight evil people with concentration power. Don't be moved by them. If they are evil, don't be evil in return. If a mad dog bites you and you bite him back, you're just a dog yourself. Evil-natured people are born with a bad temper. All you can do is ignore them and they will soon lose interest and leave."

"Oh," said Ananda, "it's really very simple."

Why did the Buddha tell Ananda to use the four words "Thus I have heard?" These four words have three meanings:

1) To distinguish Buddhist sutras from the writings of other religions. Non-Buddhist religions in India began their texts with the words "A" or "O" which means "non-existence" or "existence." As

these opposing religions see it, all dharmas in heaven and earth either exist or do not exist. "If it is not non-existent," they say, "then it exists, and if it doesn't exist, then it's non-existent." In general, as far as they can see, nothing goes beyond existence and non-existence. "In the beginning there wasn't anything," they write, "but now there is." None of these religions speaks of true emptiness and wonderful existence. Their doctrines may resemble them somewhat, but they don't explain them in detail.

Buddhist sutras are "Thus." They are just that way. The Dharma is just that way. You ask, "What is not that way?" Everything is that way. If you question it and say, "What is that way?" then nothing is that way. "Thus" is extremely wonderful. The words "Thus I have heard" distinguish Buddhist sutras from the writings of other religions.

2) To resolve the doubts of the assembly. The Buddha knew that everyone would have doubts. After the Buddha's Nirvana, while Ananda and Mahakasyapa were editing the sutras, Ananda sat on the Dharma-seat to speak the Dharma. Seeing him sitting on the Buddha's seat, the members of the assembly suddenly gave rise to three doubts:

a) Some thought, "Shakyamuni Buddha hasn't completed the stillness! He hasn't gone to Nirvana. Our Master lives!" They thought Ananda was Shakyamuni Buddha come back to life.

b) Others thought, "Shakyamuni Buddha has already entered Nirvana. This must be a Buddha from another direction: north, east, south, or west."

c) "No," said others, "the Great Master has gone to Nirvana. He hasn't come back to life, and the Buddhas of the other directions teach people in other directions. They would never come all the way to the Saha world. Why, Ananda himself must have realized Buddhahood!"

The assembly held these three doubts until Ananda said, "Thus I have heard." As soon as he said them, everyone knew that

Shakyamuni Buddha hadn't come back. They knew it was not a Buddha from another direction, and that Ananda had not become a Buddha. The Dharma which is "Thus" is that which Ananda personally heard from Shakyamuni Buddha. Three doubts suddenly arose and four words resolved them.

3) To end the assembly's debates. Of all the great Bhikshus, Ananda was the youngest. He was born on the day Shakyamuni Buddha realized Buddhahood, and when the Buddha went to Nirvana, Ananda was only forty-nine years old. Why was Ananda selected to explain and edit the sutras? Old Kasyapa was the eldest, and Maudgalyayana and Shariputra were both of higher status than Ananda. There were many others in the assembly with more Way-virtue and learning than him.

He was the youngest and it was likely that no one would believe in him and that many would try to be first. One might say, "I've heard more sutras than you so I should explain them." But when Ananda said, "Thus I have heard," everyone knew that these were not Ananda's principles, or the principles of the Great Assembly. "This is the Dharma which I, Ananda, personally heard the Buddha speak. It is not *your* teaching and not *my* teaching; it is our Master's teaching. You are not first and I am not first." This silenced the assembly's debates.

The Four Applications Of Mindfulness

1) Contemplation of the body as impure. Everyone sees his body as extremely precious. Because you think it is real, you are selfish and profit-seeking. Without a body, there would be no selfishness.

We think our bodies are real and actual. Being selfish, we create offenses and commit evil deeds. We cannot let go of the affairs of the world and calculate on behalf of our bodies all day long, looking for good food, beautiful clothes, and a nice place to live – a little happiness for the body. On the day we die, we are still unclear. "My body is dying," we moan. "How can it do this to me?" At that time we know that our bodies are unreal, but it's too late, too late for our regrets.

Ultimately, is the body real? Stupid people think so, but wise people see it merely as a combination of the four elements: earth, air, fire, and water. It is not ultimate.

"Then," you ask, "what *is* ultimate?"

> *Our own self-nature is*
> *bright and all-illumining;*
> *Our own-self-nature is*
> *perfect and unimpeded.*
> *It is nowhere and nowhere is it not;*
> *to the end of empty space,*
> *it exhausts the Dharma Realm.*

Our bodies are temporary dwellings where our self-nature comes to live for a time. But the person dwelling in the hotel is not the hotel, and in the same way, his body is not him. The traveller who thinks that he is the hotel is mistaken. If you know that the body is just like a hotel, you should seek that which dwells within it, for once you have found it, you will recognize your true self.

From the time of birth, the body is impure – a combination of its father's semen and its mother's blood. The child grows up with greed, hate, stupidity, pride, and doubt. He commits offenses, creating the karma of killing, stealing, sexual misconduct, lying and taking intoxicants and drugs. Offense-karma is created because of the body. But is the body such a precious thing after all? No.

A precious jewel is pure and undefiled, without stain or the slightest trace of filth. Our bodies, on the other hand, have nine apertures which constantly secrete impure substances: tears from the eyes, wax from the ears, mucus from the nose...

There are religions whose members eat mucus. They say that they are "smelting the cinnabar." They also eat tears and ear wax thinking that these filthy substances are precious jewels. Isn't that pitiful?

Two ears, two eyes, and two nostrils make six holes. The mouth is full of phlegm and saliva. That's seven holes. Add the anus and urinary tract and you have nine. Would you call this pure? Everyone knows that excrement and urine are unclean and, if you don't believe it, just try seasoning some fine food with a tiny pinch of excrement. No one will eat it. People will want to vomit instead because it is unclean. Would you call this body, dribbling filth from nine holes, a jewel? If it's a jewel, why do such vile things flow from it?

If you don't bathe for a week, you itch and squirm and a thick crust forms on your body. Where did it come from? Soon you stink with an odor even a dog finds repulsive. What is the advantage of having a body? Contemplate the body as impure. If you see how filthy it is, do you still love it? Are you still attached? What's the use of loving such a dirty thing?

"Then can I stab myself? Can I kill myself?" you ask.

No. That's not necessary. You must borrow this false body and use it to cultivate the Truth. The self-nature dwells within the body. You entered the body of five skandhas and the *yin* and *yang* merged in a combination of purity and filth which is your body. If you cultivate, you can go up, and attain purity. If you do not cultivate you will go down, create offense karma, unite with the filth, and turn into a ghost.

Go up. Become a Buddha. Whether or not you cultivate is up to you, however. Nobody can force you to cultivate.

The Venerable Ananda thought that because he was the Buddha's cousin, he didn't need to cultivate. He thought that the Buddha would just give him samadhi. But the Buddha couldn't do that, and so it was not until after the Buddha's Nirvana, when Ananda was about to edit the sutras, that he finally certified to the fourth Stage of Arhatship and realized that he could not neglect cultivation.

Be mindful that the body is impure, don't be so fond of it, and don't take it as a treasure.

You say, "I can't stand criticism. I can't stand it."

Who are *you*?

"If they hit me, I can't bear it. It hurts!"

Really? If you put your attachments down and see through them, there is neither pain nor not pain. Who is in pain? What, exactly, hurts? If someone hits you, pretend that you bumped into a wall. If someone scolds you, pretend that they are singing a song or speaking Japanese. How can they scold you if you don't understand them?

"Are they speaking Spanish or Portugese? French? German? I've never studied languages so I don't understand..." They can scold you, but it's nothing. In general, once you see through, break, and put down the attachment to your body, you win your independence.

Contemplate your body as impure. Don't regard it with so much importance. It's not important.

Contemplate feelings, thoughts, and dharmas as impure also.

2) Contemplate feelings as suffering. Feelings may be pleasant, unpleasant or neutral; from the point of view of the three sufferings, unpleasant feelings are the suffering within suffering, pleasant feelings are caught up in the suffering of decay, and neutral feelings are the suffering of process. Wake up! Everything you enjoy is a form of suffering. If you know that pleasure is suffering, you will not be attached to it. I often say:

Enduring suffering puts an end to suffering;
Enjoying blessings destroys blessings.

If you endure your suffering, it will pass. If you enjoy your blessings, they, too, will pass. Contemplate feelings as suffering.

The body, thought, and dharmas are also suffering. Although there are Four Applications of Mindfulness, you can divide them up; each of the four characteristic qualities, impurity, suffering, impermanence, and the absence of self, can be applied to the body, to feelings, to thoughts, and to dharmas, making sixteen applications in all.

3) Contemplate thoughts as impermanent. The *Vajra Sutra* says, "Past thought cannot be obtained, present thought cannot be obtained, and future thought cannot be obtained."

All your thoughts are unobtainable. They flow without stopping and so they are impermanent. The body, feelings, and dharmas are also impermanent.

4) Contemplate dharmas as without self. Basically, since there are no dharmas, from whence cometh the self? The self is a combination of four elements and the five skandhas – a creation of

form dharmas. Outside of the four elements and the five skandhas there is no self. So contemplate dharmas as being without a self.

The Four Applications of Mindfulness are very wonderful. If you investigate them thoroughly, understand and dwell on them, you will be unattached and will attain true freedom. If you're attached, you can't be free. Why? Because you're attached! So dwell in the Four Applications of Mindfulness. Dwell and yet do not dwell.

The Six Requirements

Ananda's fourth question concerned evil-natured Bhikshus. The Buddha said, "Be silent and they will leave." Even while the Buddha was in the world, there were evil-natured Bhikshus, laymen, and ordinary people. "If you ignore them," the Buddha said, "they will get bored and leave."

Thus I have heard. Thus fills the requirement of 1) faith. The Dharma which is **Thus** can be believed. Dharma, which is not **Thus**, cannot be believed. **I have heard** fills the requirement of 2) hearing. "Since the ears do the hearing, "you may ask, "why does it say I have heard?" This is because whereas the ears are just a small part of the body, "I" refers to the whole person. **At one time** fills the requirement of 3) time.

"Why," you may ask, "doesn't the sutra give the month, day, and year?"

Calendars differ from nation to nation. Some countries begin the year in the first month, some in the second or third month of another country's calendar. There is no one way to indicate the date, and, what is more, if the date were given, people would start doing research to determine if it was correct. Because the sutra only states, **at one time**, there is no demand for historical verification.

In order to speak the Dharma, there must be an 4) audience; in this case it was the **gathering of great Bhikshus**. The audience must also have the time to come and listen, for if they don't stay, of what use is their faith? They must have the time to listen, they must want to hear the Dharma, and they must believe in it. Then there must also be a Dharma-speaking host. In this case, the **Buddha** is the 5) host, and the 6) place is **Sravasti, in the Garden of the Benefactor of Orphans and the Solitary.** Therefore, in the opening sentences of the sutra, all six requirements are fulfilled.

Sravasti is the name of a city in India. Translated, it means "abundance and virtue,"[18] because the seven jewels: gold, silver, lapiz lazuli, crystal, mother-of-pearl, red pearls, and carnelian, and the objects of the five desires: beauty, wealth, fame, food, and sleep, were in abundance there. The people of Sravasti were very intelligent and had the virtue of great learning and liberation.

You could also say that the objects of the five desires are forms, sounds, smells, tastes, and tangibles. The states connected with the objects of the five desires turn people's wisdom upside-down. The eyes run off after forms, the ears after sounds, the nose after smell, the tongue after tastes, and the body after tangibles. Deluded people spin around and around in pursuit of the objects of the five desires.

The people of Sravasti had great learning and refinement. They were also liberated, free, and unfettered, and were only slightly attached.

---

18. *feng de* 豐德

The Benefactor's Garden

In the Jeta Grove, in the Garden of the Benefactor of Orphans and the Solitary. Anathapindada, whose name means "benefactor of orphans and the solitary,"[19] was a wealthy elder who lived in the city of Sravasti. He was also known as Sudatta, which means "joyous giving."[20] He was a rich man, but he didn't understand the Buddhadharma. In fact, he had never even heard the Buddha's name. One day, while arranging for his son's marriage, he visited a friend, the wealthy elder Shan Tan Nou.

That night Shan Tan Nou rose and began to decorate his house. Sudatta asked, "You're adorning the house so beautifully, is there to be a celebration? Is your son going to be married?"

"No," said Shan Tan Nou. "I have invited the Buddha to receive offerings."

When Sudatta heard the word "Buddha," every hair on his body stood straight up on end. "Who is the Buddha?" he gasped.

"The Buddha is the Crown Prince, son of King Suddhodana. He would have been the king, but he left home to cultivate the Way and became a Buddha instead. I have invited him here to receive offerings."

---

19. *ji gu du* 給孤獨
20. *le shi* 樂施

Having heard the word "Buddha," Sudatta couldn't get back to sleep. Shakyamuni Buddha knew that Sudatta's heart was sincere and he emitted a light which shone so brightly that Sudatta thought it was dawn, got out of bed, and went out of the city. The city gate was locked, but the Buddha opened it with his spiritual powers and Sudatta proceeded to the Buddha's dwelling in the Bamboo Grove.

Just as Sudatta arrived, four gods descended, circumambulated the Buddha three times, and then bowed in order to show Sudatta the proper gestures of respect. Because Sudatta had never seen the Buddha or heard the Dharma, he followed the gods' example and the Buddha explained the Dharma to him. Sudatta was delighted and said, "Buddha, you have so many followers, you really need a big place to live. I shall prepare one and invite you to live there."

"Fine," said the Buddha.

Sudatta looked, but he couldn't find the right land. Finally, he saw Prince Jeta's garden. It was big enough, but Prince Jeta refused to sell. "If you want to buy my garden," he laughed, "first cover it with gold coins. That's my price."

Sudatta didn't stay to bargain with him, he just said "Okay," and moved his treasury, piece by piece, to the garden and covered the entire grove. "Now your garden belongs to me," he said to Prince Jeta.

"I was only joking," said the Prince, annoyed. "I'm keeping it for myself. How could I sell it to you?"

"You told me that you would sell if I covered it with gold, and I took you at your word," Sudatta said. "If you plan to be a king, you really shouldn't joke with people. A king's word must stand."

"Very well," said the Prince, "you covered the ground with gold, so the park is yours. But you didn't cover the trees. The trees are mine! But I'll give them as a donation..."

Because the trees belonged to Prince Jeta, it is called the Jeta Grove, and because the garden was Sudatta's, it's called the Garden of the Benefactor of Orphans and the Solitary.

In China, when King Wen established the nation, he assisted four kinds of poor people: widows, widowers, orphans, and the childless, or solitary. Sudatta also gave aid to these four kinds of people, and so he is known as the Benefactor of Orphans and the Solitary, that is, Anathapindada.

Together with a gathering of great Bhikshus, twelve hundred and fifty in all. This phrase fulfills the audience requirement. **Together** means that they studied under the same teacher, lived in the same place, and investigated the Buddhadharma together. They all had the same Bodhi mind and had opened the same wisdom, attained the same result, and would together realize Buddhahood. Because they had so much in common, the text reads, **together**.

The sutra text first lists the assembly of Sound Hearers because they are sages who have transcended the world. The Bodhisattvas are listed next because they are sometimes Bhikshus and sometimes laymen. They cultivate the Middle Way and so they are listed in the middle. The gods and dragons of the eight-fold division are listed last because they are in the world and represent the common people. Sometimes the Bodhisattvas are present in the Dharma assembly, and sometimes they travel to other worlds. The Bhikshus, on the other hand, were the Buddha's constant followers. They always listened to the sutras and the Dharma, and so they are listed first.

Great has three meanings:

1) great,

2) many, and

3) victorious.

Bhikshus are respected by kings and "great" men and so they are "great." They have cut off afflictions and destroyed the "many" evils. They are different from, and "victorious" over all external religions.

Bhikshu also has three meanings:

1) seeker of almsfood,

2) one who frightens Mara, and

3) destroyer of evil.

When one ascends the precept platform to be ordained, one's request for ordination may be granted after three appeals. An earth-bound yaksa ghost informs a space-travelling yaksa, who flies up to inform the heavenly demons. The heavenly demons are terrified and tell Mara, the king of the sixth desire heaven, "The Buddha's retinue has increased by one and ours has decreased by one!" At this, Mara's palace quakes. Thus a Bhikshu is one who frightens Mara.

He also destroys the evils of the eighty-four thousand afflictions because he has resolved his mind on Bodhi.

The Six Harmonious Unities of the Sangha

These Bhikshus were assembled together as a Sangha. **Sangha** is a Sanskrit word which means "harmoniously united assembly."[21] They live together without bickering or fighting and are united in terms of phenomena and noumena. In terms of the noumenal aspect, they have given proof to liberation and to the unconditioned. In terms of the phenomenal, they are united in six ways:

1) As a harmonious group, they dwell together. They don't look at one another's faults and fight among themselves. No one has a special style. There are, for example, no solitary drinkers or smokers out of harmony with the rest. Everyone who lives with the Sangha must abide by the Sangha's rules.

2) With harmonious speech, they do not quarrel. They don't gossip. They don't say, "So and so has such and such an asset, and so and so has such and such a fault... three frogs have six eyes." Their speech is harmonious and what they talk about is important and has principle. They don't argue.

3) With harmonious thoughts, they enjoy the same things. One person likes to study the Buddhadharma and so does the next. One is vigorous and the next is even more so. The more one person cultivates, the more the next cultivates. Everyone makes vigorous

---

[21.] *huo he zhong* 和合眾

progress. Every day they are more energetic, not more lazy. Cultivating more and speaking less, their minds are in harmony.

4) With harmonious views, they have the same liberation.

5) With the same precepts, they cultivate together.

6) In harmony, they mutually share their benefits.

Twelve hundred fifty in all. These were the Buddha's constant followers, his retainers. When the Buddha went to lecture sutras, these Arhats always went along, even if they had already heard the sutra.

There were actually twelve hundred fifty-five disciples, but for the sake of convenience the number was rounded off to twelve hundred fifty. Where did the disciples come from? In the Deer Park, the Buddha first taught the five Bhikshus. Then Yasas, the son of an Elder, and his forty-nine disciples took refuge. The Venerable Shariputra and the Venerable Mahamaudgalyayana each had a hundred disciples who took refuge. That makes two hundred fifty-five. The Kasyapa Brothers had a thousand disciples, making twelve hundred fifty-five, and, rounded off, twelve hundred fifty in all.

The Kasyapa Brothers

The three Kasyapa brothers had a thousand disciples. Five hundred were with Uruvilva Kasyapa. Uruvilva means "papaya grove,"[22] for it is said that he cultivated in a papaya grove. Some accounts claim that he had a lump on his chest which resembled a papaya, some describing it as concave, and some as convex! What is probable is that, liking to eat papayas, he cultivated in a papaya grove and in time a papaya grew on his chest. Papayas are good for curing illnesses of the lungs.

Uruvilva Kasyapa had two brothers, Gaya, meaning "city"[23] or "elephant head mountain,"[24] and Nadi, meaning "river."[25] The two brothers had five hundred disciples between them, and so the three brothers had a total of one thousand disciples.

The Buddha first taught and crossed over the five Bhikshus in the Deer Park. Then he considered who to cross over next. Seeing that the potential of the three Kasyapa brothers had matured, he went to the dwelling of Uruvilva Kasyapa. He could not, however, simply say, "I have come to save you, Uruvilva Kasyapa. Do you believe that?" He had to employ a clever expedient device and so he said, "It's late and I can't travel any farther. May I stay on here?"

---

22. *mu gua lin* 木瓜林
23. *cheng* 城
24. *xiang tou shan* 象頭山
25. *he* 河

Uruvilva Kasyapa, a powerful fire worshipper, saw the Buddha and thought, "Why is he so special?" Try as he might, he couldn't figure the Buddha out. "Strange," he thought, "I can see anyone else's background just by looking. Why can't I see his?" Finally he said to the Buddha, "Very well, you may stay here," and he put him in a cave where Uruvilva Kasyapa's protector, a dragon, lived. The dragon was extremely fierce and scorched to death anyone who came near him. In the middle of the night, the dragon tried to burn the Buddha, but the Buddha had entered the fire-light samadhi and couldn't be burned. The Buddha put the dragon in his bowl. More than likely, he didn't have to trick him by saying, "You can only make fire, you can't jump into my bowl," as the Sixth Patriarch would later speak to another dragon: "You can only manifest a big body, not a small one." The Buddha used a very natural method to get the dragon into his bowl. Then he explained the Dharma to him and the dragon took refuge.

Seeing such spiritual penetrations and transformation, Kasyapa knew that his own virtue was not as great as the Buddha's. Thereupon, he took refuge and instructed his five hundred disciples to do the same. Soon after leaving home, they gave proof to the sagely fruit.

Kasyapa's two brothers were also fire-worshippers, but when they saw that their brother had become a Bhikshu, they wanted to leave home as well. They did, and, along with their five hundred disciples, they soon gave proof to the sagely fruit.

That makes one thousand two hundred and fifty-five disciples. Out of gratitude for the Buddha's deep kindness and his teaching, they were the Buddha's constant followers. No matter where the Buddha went, they accompanied him and protected the assembly. For example, here we lecture on the sutras and those who come to listen protect the assembly. Even though they already understand the doctrines, they still take time from their busy schedules to come and listen.

All great Arhats whom the assembly knew and recognized. Arhat, a Sanskrit word, has three meanings which correspond to the three meanings of the word Bhikshu, because being a Bhikshu is the cause of attaining Arhatship, and Arhatship is the result of cultivation as a Bhikshu. It's a matter of cause and effect.

An Arhat is:

1) Worthy of offerings. On the causal ground, a Bhikshu is a seeker of alms food, and in the result he is worthy of the offerings of gods and men.

2) One without birth. A Bhikshu frightens Mara, and in the result, as an Arhat, he undergoes no further birth.

3) A slayer of thieves. On the causal ground, a Bhikshu destroys evil, and in the result, as an Arhat, he has slain the thieves of ignorance and affliction.

On the causal ground, the Bhikshu frightens the demons of the five skandhas, the afflictions, and death. Death is also a demon. Some cultivators practice diligently, yet when they fall sick and confront death, they are afraid. "I'm going to die!" they cry, turned by the demon of death. Real cultivators fear nothing. They are not afraid of life and they are not afraid of death. Life and death are the same. Death and life are not different. There is no distinction between them. If while alive cultivators can be as if dead, they will have no thoughts of desire. How can one have desire, greed, hate, stupidity, pride, or doubt as a dead man? When one arrives at this state there are no afflictions, no troubles at all. This is true happiness.

This state is not easy to attain, however, on the other hand, it is not difficult either. If you want to, you can do it.

For example, when one of my disciples became extremely sick, he said to me repeatedly, "I'm really suffering."

I said, "The more suffering you undergo, the better. The more you suffer the more you will understand."

One day it seemed as if he had died. He went to a happy place full of people. "Happiness is happiness," he said, "but I want to see my teacher."

"Who is your teacher?" the people asked.

As soon as they heard his teacher's name they were unhappy. "You can't see your teacher here," they said.

"Then I'm leaving," he said, and came back; he didn't die after all. You might say he has conquered the demon of death. Subsequently, his skill has increased greatly.

Whom the assembly knew and recognized. These arhats were all very famous and their virtue was respected by the entire population. Everyone knew their names and recognized their faces.

The Assembly of Arhats

Elders Shariputra, Mahamaudgalyayana, Mahakasyapa, Mahakatyayana, Mahakausthila, Revata, Suddhipanthaka, Nanda, Ananda, Rahula, Gavampati, Pindola Bharadvaja, Kalodayin, Mahakapphina, Vakkula, Aniruddha, and others such as these, all great disciples;

Commentary:

Elder is a term used to show respect for another's position. There are three kinds of elders:

1) Elders in age,
2) Elders in the Dharma Nature,
3) Elders in blessings and virtue.

An elder in age has lived for many years. A Dharma Nature elder understands the Buddhadharma and comprehends his self-nature; regardless of his age, he is nonetheless an elder in terms of his wisdom and intelligence. One such as this may be young in years, but he can lecture on sutras and speak the Dharma. His wisdom is limitless and his eloquence is unobstructed. Elders in blessings and virtue are fortunate because people like to make offerings to them. Because of their virtuous conduct they are fields where, by making offerings, one plants the causes of future blessings.

Shariputra

Shariputra was a Dharma Nature elder. At the age of eight he studied and mastered all the Buddhadharma in only seven days, and he could out-debate all the Indian philosophers. His name is Sanskrit. His father's name was Tisya and his mother's name was Sarika. Hence he was known as Upatisya, "Little Tisya," and as Shariputra, the Son (*putra*) of *Sari*.

The word *Shariputra* may be translated three ways,

1) "Body son"[26] because his mother's body was extremely beautiful, and her features very refined;

2) "Egret son"[27] due to his mother's eyes which were as beautiful as an egret's and,

3) "Jewel son"[28] because her eyes shone like jewels. Shariputra's mother's eyes were beautiful, and when she bore this jewel-eyed son, his eyes were beautiful, too.

He was the foremost of the Sravakas in wisdom. While still in the womb, he helped his mother debate, and she always won. In the past, whenever she had debated with her brother, she had always lost; but while she was pregnant with Shariputra, her brother always lost.

"This isn't your own power," he said. "The child in your womb must be incredibly intelligent. He is helping you debate and that's why I lost." Thereupon he decided to study logic and travelled to Southern India where he studied for many years.

---

26. *shen zi* 身子
27. *chou lu zi* 鶖鷺子
28. *zhu zi* 珠子

There was no electricity at that time yet, but he studied by day and by night. He mastered the Four Vedas, the classics of Indian knowledge, without wasting a moment. He didn't take time to mend his tattered clothing, wash his face, or even cut his nails which grew so long that everyone called him "The Long-Nailed Brahmin."

Having mastered various philosophical theories, he returned to debate with his sister's son. He had spent a great deal of time preparing for the event, and felt that if he lost it would be the height of disgrace. "Where is your son?" he asked his sister.

"Shariputra has left the home-life under the Buddha," she said.

The Long-Nailed Brahmin was displeased. "How could he?' he said. "What virtue does the Buddha have? He's just a Sramana. Why should anyone follow him? I'm going to go bring my nephew back."

He went to the Buddha and demanded his nephew, but the Buddha said, "Why do you want him back? You can't just casually walk off with him. Establish your principles and I'll consider your request."

"I take non-accepting as my doctrine," said the uncle.

"Really?" said the Buddha. "Do you accept your view of non-accepting? Do you accept your doctrine or not?"

Now the uncle had just said that he didn't accept anything. But when the Buddha asked him whether or not he accepted his own view of non-accepting, he could hardly admit he accepted it for that would invalidated his doctrine of non-acceptance. But if he said that he didn't accept it, he would contradict his own statement of his doctrine and his view. He was therefore unable to answer either way.

Before the debate, he had made an agreement with the Buddha that if he won he would take his nephew, but if he lost, he said that he would cut off his head and give it to the Buddha.

The uncle had bet his head and lost. So what did he do? He ran!

About four miles down the road he stopped and thought, "I can't run away. I told the Buddha that if I lost he could have my head. I'm a man, after all, and I should keep my word. It's unmanly to run away." Then he returned to Shakyamuni Buddha and said, "Give me a knife, I'm going to cut off my head!"

"What for?" said the Buddha.

"I lost, didn't I? I owe you my head, don't I?" he said.

"There's no such principle in my Dharma," said the Buddha. "Had you won, you could have taken your nephew, but since you lost, why don't you leave home instead?"

"Will you accept me?" he said.

"Yes," replied the Buddha.

So not only did the nephew not return, but the uncle didn't return home either.

At age eight, the Great, Wise Shariputra had penetrated the Real Mark of all dharmas in only seven days, and defeated all the philosophers in India. When Shakyamuni Buddha spoke the *Amitabha Sutra* without request, Shariputra was at the head of the assembly, because only wisdom such as his could comprehend the deep, wonderful doctrine of the Pure Land Dharma Door.

Not only was he foremost in wisdom, he was not second in spiritual penetrations either. Once a layman invited the Buddha to receive offerings. Shariputra had entered samadhi, and no matter how they called to him, he wouldn't come out. He wasn't being obnoxious by showing off, thinking, "I hear them, but I'm not moving, that's all there is to it." No, he had really entered samadhi.

When he didn't respond to the bell, Maudgalyayana, foremost in spiritual powers, applied every bit of strength he had, but couldn't move him. He couldn't even ruffle the corner of his robe. This proves that Shariputra was not only number one in wisdom, but also in spiritual penetrations. He wasn't like us. If someone bumps us while we sit in meditation, we know it. Shariputra had real samadhi.

We should look into this: Why was Shariputra foremost in wisdom? Why was he called "The Greatly Wise Shariputra?" It's a matter of cause and effect. In a former life, in the causal ground, when he first decided to study, he met a teacher who asked him, "Would you like to be intelligent?"

"Yes I would," said Shariputra.

"Then study the dharma-door of Prajna wisdom. Recite the Great Compassion Mantra, the Shurangama Mantra, the Ten Small Mantras, and the *Heart Sutra*.[29] Recite them every day and your wisdom will unfold."

Shariputra followed his teacher's instructions and recited day and night, while standing, sitting, walking, and reclining. He didn't recite for just one day, but made a vow to recite continuously, to bow to his teacher, and to study the Buddhadharma life after life. Life after life, he studied Prajna, and life after life his wisdom increased until, when Shakyamuni Buddha appeared in the world, Shariputra was able to penetrate the Real Mark of all dharmas in only seven days.

Who was his former teacher? Just Shakyamuni Buddha! When Shakyamuni Buddha realized Buddhahood, Shariputra became an Arhat, and because he obeyed his teacher, he had great wisdom. He never forgot the doctrines his teacher taught him, and so, in seven days, he mastered all the Buddha's dharmas.

When one has not studied very much Buddhadharma in the past, one learns mantras and sutras slowly. One may recite the Shurangama mantra for months and still be unable to recite it from memory. It is most important, however, not to be lazy. Be vigorous and diligent. Like Shariputra, don't relax day or night. Those who can't remember should study hard, and those who can should increase their efforts and enlarge their wisdom. You should consider, "Why is my wisdom so much less than everyone else's? Why is his wisdom so lofty and mine so unclear? Why do I

---

29. These are recited daily in Buddhist temples for morning recitation.

understand so little? It's because I haven't studied the Buddha-dharma." Now that we have met the Dharma we should vow to study it. Then in the future we can run right past Shariputra and study with the Greatly Wise Bodhisattva Manjushri, who is far, far wiser than the Arhat Shariputra. This is the cause behind Shariputra's wisdom, a useful bit of information.

Three American Shramanera and two American Shramanerika have now received the complete precepts: Shramanera, Bhikshu, and Bodhisattva Precepts. You could say that they are new Bodhisattvas returning to America. People who have received the Bodhisattva precepts cultivate the Bodhisattva Way, and people who have received the Bhikshu precepts uphold the Buddhadharma and teach living beings. When these five return from Taiwan, we Americans should protect them as precious treasures. All of you should be their Dharma protectors for they are returning to America to establish American Buddhism so that in the future, Americans will be able to cultivate and realize Buddhahood. This is my hope.

Mahamaudgalyayana

The Sanskrit word *Maha* has three meanings:

1) great,
2) many, and
3) victorious.

As an elder, one is respected by many kings and great ministers. Having studied the sutras in the Tripitaka, an elder has victoriously transcended all non-Buddhist religions.

Maudgalyayana is Sanskrit and means "descendent of a family of bean gatherers."[30] His name also means "turnip root"[31] because his ancestors ate turnips when they cultivated the Way. He is also

---

[30] *cai shu shi* 采菽氏
[31] *lai fu* 萊菔

called "Kolita" after the tree where his father and mother prayed to the spirit of that tree for a son.

This Venerable One was the foremost in spiritual penetrations. In his cultivation of the Way, when he first certified to Arhatship, he obtained six kinds of spiritual penetrations: the heavenly eye, the heavenly ear, the knowledge of others' thoughts, the knowledge of past lives, the extinction of outflows, and the complete spirit. With the heavenly eye, one sees not only the affairs of men, but every action of the gods as well. With the heavenly ear, one hears the gods speaking. With the knowledge of others' thoughts, one knows what others are thinking and planning before they speak. With the knowledge of past lives, not only does one know what they are thinking, but one clearly knows their causes and effects from former lives.

As to the extinction of outflows, all people have outflows. They are like leaky bottles: pour something in the top and it flows out the bottom. The bigger the hole, the faster the flow. The smaller the hole, the slower the flow. If there are no holes, there are no leaks, no outflows. The extinction of outflows is the absence of leaks.

What outflows do people have? Food and drink become the outflows of feces and urine. If you like to get angry, that's an outflow. If you are greedy, hateful, or stupid, you have outflows. Pride and doubt are outflows, too.

With outflows, nothing can be retained, but without them, all leaks disappear. Outflows are simply our faults. People! If we don't have big sicknesses, we have small sicknesses, and if we don't have small sicknesses, we have little faults. If we don't have big outflows, we have small outflows, and if we don't have small outflows, we have slow leaks, little bad habits. A lot can be said about outflows. The absence of them is called the Penetration of the Extinction of Outflows.

The Penetration of the Complete Spirit is also called the "penetration of the realm of the spirit" and the "spiritual penetration of everything as you will it to be." The complete spirit means that you have an inconceivable power. Not even the ghosts and spirits can know of your thousand changes and ten thousand transformations, for you have penetrated all realms and states without obstruction. "As you will" means that everything is the way you want it. If you want to go to the heavens, you go; if you want to go down into the earth, you go. You can walk into the water without drowning, and into the fire without burning. If you're in your room and think, "I'd rather not go out the door," you can walk right through the wall. How can this be? It's "as you will" according to your thought. However you think you would like it to be, that's the way it is. You just have to make a wish and you attain your aim. These are the Six Spiritual Penetrations.

When Mahamaudgalyayana first obtained these penetrations, he looked for his father and mother. Not so much his father, actually, as his mother. Where was she? His mother was in hell. Why? Because she had not believed in the Triple Jewel: the Buddha, the Dharma, and the Sangha; and what is more, she had slandered them. She had also eaten fish eggs and flesh, and thereby had killed many beings.

Seeing her in hell, Maudgalyayana sent her a bowl of food. She took it in one hand and hid it with the other because she was afraid the other hungry ghosts would see it and try to steal it from her. Being greedy herself, she knew that other hungry ghosts were greedy too, and so she covered it over stealthily.

Although it was good food, her heavy karmic obstacles prevented her from eating it. When the food reached her mouth it turned into flaming coals which burned her lips. Maudgalyayana's spiritual powers could not prevent the food from turning into fire, so he asked the Buddha to help him.

The Buddha told him to save his mother by arranging an Ullambana offering. Ullambana means, "releasing those who are hanging upside down." The Buddha told Maudgalyayana that, on the fifteenth day of the seventh (lunar) month, the day of the Buddha's delight and the monks' Pravarana he should offer all varieties of food and drink to the Sangha of the ten directions. In this way he could rescue his mother so she could leave suffering and obtain bliss.

Maudgalyayana followed these instructions and his mother was reborn in the heavens. Not only was his mother saved, but all the hungry ghosts in the hells simultaneously left suffering and attained bliss.

Now, you may say, "I don't believe that food and drink become fire when hungry ghosts eat them." Of course you don't believe it! But the world is full of strange, strange things. It would be hard to speak about them all. How much the less can one be clear about those things beyond this world. Let's take water, for example. People and animals see water as water, but the gods see it as lapis lazuli and the hungry ghosts see it as fire. It's all a question of individual karmic manifestations. Gods have the karmic retribution of gods, men of men, and ghosts of ghosts.

This is how, with the Buddha's help, Maudgalyayana saved his mother.

Mahakasyapa

Again, *Maha* means great, many, and victorious. The Sanskrit word *Kasyapa* means "great turtle clan,"[32] because Mahakasyapa's ancestors saw the pattern on the back of a giant turtle and used it to cultivate the Way.

Kasyapa also means, "light drinking clan,"[33] because his body shone with a light which was so bright it seemed to "drink up" all other light.

Why did his body shine? Seven Buddhas ago, in the time of the Buddha Vipasyin, there was a poor woman who decided to repair a ruined temple. The roof of the temple had been blown off and the

---

[32.] *da gui shi* 大龜氏
[33.] *yin guang shi* 飲光氏

images inside were exposed to the wind and rain. The woman went everywhere and asked for help, and when she had collected enough money she commissioned a goldsmith to regild the images. By the time he was finished, the goldsmith fell in love with her and said, "You have attained great merit from this work, but we should share it. You may supply the gold and I will furnish the labour, free." So the temple was rebuilt and the images regilded. The goldsmith asked the woman to marry him and, in every life, for ninety-one kalpas, they were husband and wife and their bodies shone with purple and golden light.

Mahakasyapa was born in India, in Magadha. When he was twenty his father and mother wanted him to marry, but he said, "The woman I marry must shine with golden light. Unless you find such a woman, I won't marry." Eventually they found one, and they were married. As a result of their good karma their bodies shone with gold light and they cultivated together and investigated the doctrines of the Way. When Mahakasyapa left home to become a Bhikshu, his wife became a Bhikshuni called "Purple and Golden Light."

Mahakasyapa's personal name was "Pippala," because his parents prayed to the spirit of a pippala tree to grant them a son.

As the First Patriarch, Mahakasyapa holds an important position in Buddhism. When Shakyamuni Buddha spoke the Dharma, the Great Brahma Heaven King presented him with a golden lotus and Shakyamuni Buddha held up the flower before the assembly. At that time, hundreds of thousands of gods and men were present, but no one responded except Mahakasyapa, who simply smiled. Then the Buddha said, "I have the Right Dharma-Eye Treasury. The wonderful Nirvanic mind, the Real Mark which is unmarked. This dharma-door of mind to mind transmission has been transmitted to Kasyapa." Thus Mahakasyapa received the transmission of Dharma and became the first Buddhist Patriarch.

Venerable Mahakasyapa is still present in the world. When he left home under the Buddha he was already one hundred and sixty years old. By the time Shakyamuni Buddha had spoken Dharma for forty-nine years in over three hundred Dharma assemblies, Kasyapa was already over two hundred years old. After Shakyamuni Buddha entered Nirvana, Kasyapa went to Southwestern China, to Chicken Foot Mountain in Yunnan Province. It has been over three thousand years since the Buddha's Nirvana, but Mahakasyapa is still sitting in samadhi in Chicken Foot Mountain waiting for Maitreya Buddha to appear in the world. At that time he will give Maitreya the bowl which the Four Heavenly Kings gave Shakyamuni Buddha and which Shakyamuni Buddha gave him, and his work in this world will be finished.

Many cultivators travel to Chicken Foot Mountain to worship the Patriarch Kasyapa, and on the mountain there are always three kinds of light: Buddha light, gold light, and silver light. Those with sincere hearts can hear a big bell ringing inside the mountain. It rings by itself, and although you can't see it, you can hear it for several hundred miles. It's an inconceivable state.

Mahakasyapa was the foremost of the Buddha's disciples both in ascetic practices and in age. None of the Buddha's disciples was older and none of them endured more suffering.

The term "ascetic practice"[34] means, "making an effort, raising up one's spirits with courage and vigor." The cultivation of the twelve kinds of ascetic practices is a sign that the Buddhadharma is being maintained, for as long as they are practiced, the Dharma will remain in the world. If they are not practiced, the Buddhadharma will disappear. Of the twelve ascetic practices, the first two deal with clothing:

1) Wearing rag-robes. One gathers unwanted cloth from garbage heaps, washes it, and sews it into a robe. There are many advantages in wearing rag-robes. First of all, they decrease greed. When you wear them, your heart is peaceful and calm. They also prevent others from being greedy. If you wear fine, expensive

---

[34] *ku hang* 苦行, *duskara-carya*

clothes, others may become envious and may even try to steal them. But no one wants to steal rag-robes. So the first ascetic practice benefits you and others. Those who have left home are called "tattered sons" because they wear rag-robes.

2) Wearing only three robes. One's only possessions are three robes, a bowl, and a sitting cloth. The first robe is the great robe, the *samghati*, made of 25 strips of cloth in 108 patches, which is worn when lecturing sutras or visiting the king. The second is the outer robe, the *uttarasanga*, made of seven pieces, which is worn when bowing repentance ceremonies and worshipping the Buddha. The third is the inner robe in five pieces, the *antarvasaka*, which is worn at all times, to work in, to travel in, and to entertain guests. With only three robes, a bowl, and a sitting cloth, one teaches others to be content and not be greedy for a lot of possessions.

3) Always begging for food. One always takes one's bowl to beg, and does not cook for oneself.

4) Begging in succession. One begs from house to house in regular order without discriminating between the rich and the poor. If, by the seventh house, no food is obtained, one doesn't eat on that day. One doesn't think, "I want to beg from the poor, not the rich," or "I want to beg from the rich and not the poor."

Mahakasyapa once said, "Poor people are to be pitied. If they don't plant blessings now, in the future they will be even poorer." He begged exclusively from the poor.

Subhuti, on the other hand, begged only from the rich. "If they are rich," he reasoned, "we should help them continue to plant blessings and meritorious virtue. If they don't make offerings to the Triple Jewel, next life they'll have no money," and so he begged only from the rich.

But the Buddha scolded both of them. "You two have the hearts of Arhats," he said, "because you discriminate in your begging." To beg properly, one should go from house to house, without discrimination.

5) Eating only once in the middle of the day. This means that you do not eat in the morning or in the evening, but only between the hours of eleven and twelve o'clock in the morning. Some who don't understand the Buddhadharma think that "eating once in the middle of the day" means simply eating only one lunch. It actually means that one doesn't eat in the morning or in the evening, but only once in the middle of the day. In China, when one receives the precepts, they ask, "Neng chi?" which means "Can you keep them?" The preceptee answers, "Neng chi!" which means "I can." If one eats in the morning, noon, and evening, however, one can answer "Neng chi!" which sounds the same, but means "I can eat!"

Eating once a day at noon is one of the Buddha's rules, because the Buddha only responded to offerings of food at noon. Gods eat in the morning, animals eat in the afternoon, and ghosts eat at night. Those who have left home do not eat at night because when ghosts come out at night to look for food and hear the sound of chopsticks they run to steal the food. The food the people are eating turns into fire in the ghosts' mouths and they get angry and take revenge by making people sick.

6) Reducing the measure of what you eat. If you can eat three bowls, then eat only two and a half. If you can eat two bowls, then eat only one and a half. Always eat a little less. If you eat too much your stomach can't hold it and you'll have to do a lot of work on the toilet. Eat less.

7) Not drinking juices after noon. After twelve, you don't drink apple juice, orange juice, milk, or any kind of juice at all, how much the less bean curd broth! True ascetics don't drink juice after noon.

Some people cultivate one or two of these practices and some cultivate more; some cultivate only one and some cultivate all twelve. It's not fixed; it depends upon how strong you are.

Since cultivators can't avoid the questions of clothing, food, and dwelling, these twelve ascetic practices have been established to deal with them. The five which concern dwelling are:

8) Dwelling in an *aranya*. Aranya is a Sanskrit word which means "still and quiet place."[35] In an aranya, one is left alone and there are no distracting noises. It is said,

> *What the eyes don't see*
>   *won't cause the mouth to water;*
> *What the ears don't hear*
>   *won't cause the mind to transgress.*

When people see food, they give rise to desire for it and their mouths water. If your ears don't hear confusing sounds, there is no affliction in your mind. In a still, quiet place, it is easy to cultivate diligently and enter samadhi.

9) Dwelling at the foot of a tree. You live beneath a tree, but not under any one tree for more than three nights. After two nights, you move for fear that someone might come and make offerings to you. Cultivating ascetics don't like to have such Dharma affinities or a lot of food and drink, and so they live under a tree.

10) Dwelling under the open sky. You don't live in a house or even under a tree, but right out in the open, meditating.

11) Dwelling in a graveyard. Living here, one is always on the alert. "Look at them! They're dead. In the future I'll be just like them. If I don't cultivate the Way, what will I do when it's time to die? I'll die all muddled." Dwelling in a graveyard is a good cure for laziness.

12) Ribs not touching the mat. This means always sitting and never lying down, cultivating vigorously and not fearing suffering.

These are the five ascetic practices which deal with dwelling.

Mahakasyapa cultivated not only one ascetic practice, but all twelve of them very thoroughly. Once, the Buddha moved over and asked him to sit beside him. The Buddha couldn't bear to see him cultivating ascetic practices at his age. "Kasyapa," he said, "you are

---

[35] *ji jing chu* 寂靜處

over two hundred years old, too old for ascetic practices. Take it easy. You can't endure them."

The Venerable Kasyapa smiled. He didin't say whether or not he would obey the Buddha's instructions, but he returned and continued to practices just as before. The Buddha knew this and was extremely pleased. "Because, within my Dharma, Mahakasyapa cultivates ascetic practices," he said, "the Dharma will remain long in the world. He's a great asset, foremost in asceticism."

The twelve ascetic practices are cultivated by those who have left the home-life.

"I haven't left the home-life," someone says. "Why are you explaining them to me?"

This seems like a good question, but if you look into it, it's really irrelevant. Why? Perhaps you have not left home in this life, but how do you know that you did not leave home in a past life and cultivate these practices? Perhaps you have just forgotten, and so I am reminding you.

Even if you did not leave home in past lives, perhaps next life the opportunity will arise, and the Bodhi seeds planted in this life will mature. Then your merit and virtue will be perfected and you will feel very comfortable practicing asceticism. Because you heard about it in this life, next life you will enjoy cultivating it. Perhaps in the past you planted good causes, and now you reap the good fruit; or perhaps in this life you plant good causes, and in a future life will reap the good fruit. No one can say that someone will always leave home, or that someone else will always be at home, or that someone will always be a common person. Common people all have the opportunity to realize Buddhahood. In the future these twelve ascetic practices will be of great use.

Mahakatyayana

Maha has been explained. *Katyayana* means "literary elegance,"[36] because of all the Buddha's disciples, this Venerable One was the foremost in debate. No one could defeat him. On one occasion a non-Buddhist who believed in annihilationism said, "Buddhists speak of the revolving wheel of the six paths of rebirth and maintain that after death one may be reborn again as a person, but this principle is incorrect. Why? If people can come back as people, why hasn't anyone ever died and then returned home, or sent a letter to his family? There's no basis for such a view. When people die, they go out like a lamp and they can't be born again. Buddhists imagine that there's rebirth, but actually there is none."

Mahakatyayana replied, "You've asked why those who die do not return. Before I answer first let me ask you a question. If someone were put in jail for a crime, could he return home at his convenience?"

"No," said the non-Buddhist, "of course not."

Katyayana continued, "When people descend to rebirth in the hells, it's just the same and they can't return; in fact, they are even less free to leave."

The non-Buddhist said, "Granted that those born in the hells cannot return, still, those born in the heavens are very free. Why has none of them ever sent a letter home informing his family of his whereabouts?"

Katyayana said, "What you say has principle, but, by way of analogy, suppose someone slipped and fell into a toilet, not a flush toilet – obviously no one could fall into a flush toilet – but into a pit toilet about as big as a bedroom. Once he got out, would he decide he liked the aroma there and jump back in again?"

"Heavens no," exclaimed the non-Buddhist.

---

36. *wen shi* 文飾

"The world of men," said Katyayana, "is just like a toilet, and birth in the heavens is like getting out. That's why no one comes back. Even if they did, there's the time difference to consider. For example, one day and night in the Heaven of the Thirty-Three is equal to one hundred years in the world of men. Born there, it would take a couple of days to find a place to stay and get settled, and by the time one returned on the third day, one's friends would have long been dead."

Thus, Mahakatyayana's eloquence defeated non-Buddhists who were attached to the idea of annihilation or permanence; they lost every time.

Katyayana's name also means "fan cord."[37] Soon after he was born his father died and his mother wanted to remarry, but the child was a tie, like a fan cord, which prevented her from doing so. He is also called "good shoulders"[38] because his shoulders were beautiful, and "victorious thinker"[39] because his eloquence was unobstructed.

There are four kinds of unobstructed eloquence:

1) With "unobstructed eloquence in Dharma" one can explain the Dharma without obstacle.

2) With "unobstructed eloquence in meaning" one can explain the Dharma's limitless meanings.

3) With "unobstructed eloquence in phrasing" one's rhetoric is effective.

4) With "the eloquence of unobstructed delight in speech" one takes delight in explaining the Dharma.

Because he had these four kinds of unobstructed eloquence, Mahakatyayana was the foremost of the Buddha's disciples in debate.

---

[37] *shan sheng* 扇繩
[38] *hao jian* 好肩
[39] *si sheng* 思勝

Mahakausthila

Mahakausthila was Shariputra's maternal uncle. His name means "big knees,"[40] because big knees ran in the family. He, too, was gifted in debate. In order to defeat his nephew, he went to Southern India to study non-Buddhist debating theories, rushing through his meals and gulping down water, studying so hard that he didn't even take time to wash his face or cut his nails. His nails grew so long, in fact, that he was nick-named, "The long-nailed Brahmin."

Revata

Revata means "constellation."[41] He was named after the fourth of the twenty-eight constellations, "the house, the rabbit, and the sun,"[42] because his parents prayed to this constellation in order to have their son.

Revata also means "false unity."[43] One day he went walking. When it got dark, he was far from home and decided to spend the night in a shack beside the road. Just as he was about to fall asleep two ghosts walked in, a big ghost and a small ghost. The big ghost was really big, with a green face, red hair, and a huge mouth with six teeth hanging like elephants' tusks from it. One look at him would have scared you to death! The little ghost was even uglier. His eyes, ears, nose, and mouth had all moved to the middle of his face.

The two came in dragging a corpse, and asked Revata, "What do you think? Should we eat this corpse or not?" What they meant was, "If you tell us to eat the corpse, we'll eat you instead. If you tell us not to eat the corpse, we won't have anything to eat, and so

---

40. *da xi* 大膝
41. *xing su* 星宿
42. *fang ri tu* 房日兔
43. *jia huo he* 假和合

we'll have to eat you." The ghosts were going to eat him no matter what he said.

Revata didn't say a word. The big ghost bit off the corpse's legs and the little ghost ripped off Revata's legs and stuck them on the corpse. Then the ghost ate the corpse's arms and the little ghost ripped off Revata's arms and stuck them on the corpse. The big ghost ate the entire corpse and the little ghost replaced its parts, one by one, with parts of Revata's body.

Revata then thought, "My body has been used to repair the corpse and so now I don't have a body!" The next day he ran screaming down the road asking everyone he met, "Hey! Take a look. Do I have a body?"

"What?" they said. The townspeople had no idea what he was talking about, but he kept pestering them until, finally, no one would come near him. "He's nuts," they said.

Finally Revata met two High Masters. "Shramanas," he asked, "do I have a body?"

The two High Masters happened to be Arhats. Seeing that Revata's potential for enlightenment was nearly mature, and that he would soon certify to the Dharmabody, they instructed him saying, "The body is basically created by a combination of causes and conditions. When the causes and conditions separate, the body is destroyed. There is nothing that *is* you and nothing that *is not* you." Just as they said this, "Ah!" Revata was enlightened. He left home and certified to the fruit and thus his name means, "false unity." Of the Buddha's disciples he is foremost in being "not upset or confused."

Suddhipanthaka

Suddhipanthaka and Mahapanthaka were brothers. Suddhipanthaka's name means "little roadside,"[44] and his big brother's name

---

[44] *xiao ji lu* 小繼路, "suddhi", apparently represents *ksudra*, "small."

means "big roadside." In India it is the custom for women who are about to give birth to return to their parents' home. But Mahapanthaka's mother didn't want to go home and so she waited until the last minute to leave. Consequently, her son was born on the side of the road.

When the time came to give birth to her second child, she should have known better, but again she waited. It happened again, and the second child was called "Little Roadside."

Although born in similar circumstances, the two brothers were very different in nature. The older brother was remarkably intelligent, but the younger one was remarkably... stupid. He was so stupid that he couldn't even remember half a line of verse.

The Buddha had instructed five hundred Arhats to teach him a verse, and they took turns day and night trying to teach him:

Guard your mouth, unite your mind,
With your body, don't offend.
Do not annoy a single living being.
Stay far away from non-beneficial bitter practices.
Conduct like this can surely save the world.

The three karmas of body, mouth, and mind should be pure. Do not cause others to be afflicted, and don't cultivate ascetic practices which are not in accord with Dharma. These non-beneficial bitter practices include maintaining the morality of dogs or cows, worshipping fire, sleeping in ashes, and sleeping or sitting on beds of nails, which, of course, hurts a lot. One who cultivates virtue and at the same time avoids these meaningless practices can truly save the world.

For many days, the five hundred Arhats combined their great spiritual powers trying to teach Little Roadside the verse. They taught him over and over, over and over, and he forgot it. "Recite the verse," they would say.

"But I can't remember it," Little Roadside would answer.

Finally his brother scolded him. "You're good for nothing!" he shouted. "You can't leave home. You're useless!" and he chased him away.

Little Roadside may not have had much of a memory, but he certainly had a temper. "If you won't let me leave home," he shouted, "I'll show you! I'll kill myself!" He grabbed a rope, ran to the back yard, and climbed a tree, ready to hang himself.

At that moment Shakyamuni Buddha transformed himself into a tree spirit and explained the Dharma to him. "Your brother is your brother," he said, "and you are you. He says you can't leave home, but you don't have to listen. You can cultivate right here. Why should you kill yourself?"

"That makes sense," sniffed Little Roadside. "He's he and I'm me. He has no right to tell me I can't leave home."

"Right!" said Shakyamuni Buddha. "Since you can't remember half a line, I'll give you two words, 'sweep clean.' Remember these two words, and use them to sweep your heart clean. Sweep the floor and sweep your heart free from dust."

Little Roadside said, "Yes, I'll sweep my heart. Sweep... what?"

"Clean," said the Buddha, "sweep clean."

"Oh yes," said Little Roadside. "Clean... what was the first word again?"

"Sweep," smiled the Buddha.

"Sweep clean!" said Little Roadside and he recited and swept remembering the Buddha's instructions to sweep his heart clean. In less than a week all of a sudden he was enlightened, understood everything very clearly, penetrated the Real Mark of all Dharmas, and was even more intelligent than his brother.

Little Roadside wasn't like us. We recite "Namo Amitabha Buddha" everyday, but the more we recite the more false thinking we have. If stupid people work hard and cultivate, they also can become enlightened. Don't say, "I'm too stupid to understand the sutras." If you don't understand them, don't read them; it will suffice to contemplate your heart, for when you have seen it clearly you will be enlightened. How should you contemplate your own heart? Watch for false thinking, and sweep it out of your heart. Then you can be enlightened.

Little Roadside, stupid as he was, became enlightened. We are all much more intelligent than he, and could no doubt remember "sweep clean" hearing it only once. So don't cheat yourself or take yourself lightly. Go forward bravely and study the Buddhadharma.

Were I to speak the most wonderful Dharma, unless you believed it, it would be of no use to you. But were I to speak utter nonsense, should you actually practice, it would be wonderful Dharma. If you don't practice the wonderful Dharma, it is not wonderful for you. You must always make vigorous progress. Don't fall behind or get lazy. This is most important, for if you can always make progress, the day will certainly come when you will recognize your original face.

Nanda

There were three disciples with the name "Nanda": Ananda, Sundarananda, and Nanda. Nanda, whose name means "wholesome bliss"[45] was a cow-herd before he heard the Buddha speak and decided to leave the home life. He is to be distinguished from Ananda, the Buddha's first cousin, and Sundarananda, the Buddha's little brother.

Before leaving the home-life, Nanda was a cow-herd. When he listened to the Buddha preach the Eleven Matters of Tending Cows, using the tending of cows as an analogy for cultivation of the Way, Nanda knew that the Buddha was possessed of All-Knowledge and he resolved to leave home and soon attained the fruit of Arhatship.

---

45. *shan huan xi* 善歡喜

On one occasion the Buddha instructed Nanda to preach to a group of five hundred Bhikshunis. Hearing him speak, they all attained Arhatship. In the past, the five hundred Bhikshunis had been the concubines of a king. The king was a great Dharma protector and he built a large pagoda in honor of a Buddha. The concubines believed in the Buddha and made daily offerings at the pagoda, vowing that they would in the future all obtain liberation with the king. The king was a former incarnation of Nanda.

Sundarananda

Sundarananda was the Buddha's little brother. He loved his wife, Sundari, more than anything. The two of them were as if glued together; walking, standing, sitting, and lying down, they were never apart. One day as the Buddha returned from the palace where he had gone to collect alms, he passed Sundari and Nanda who were having lunch. When he saw the Buddha, he went out to fill his bowl. As he left, Sundari spit on the floor and said, "You may give the Buddha food, but if you don't return before that dries, you're in trouble."

"Okay," said Sundarananda, and off he went. What do you think the Buddha did? Every time Sundarananda took a step forward to hand the Buddha his bowl, the Buddha moved away with his spiritual powers so that, in what seemed like just a few steps, Sundarananda suddenly found himself in the Jeta Grove, five miles from home. As soon as they arrived, the Buddha shaved Sundarananda's head. Sundarananda had no desire to leave the home-life because he did not want to give up his wife. But the Buddha was his older brother and so he complied. "You can cut off my hair," he thought, "but the first chance I get, I'm going to run away."

As day after day went by, Sundarananda got more and more nervous. The Buddha and the Arhats were staying in the Jeta Grove, and Sundarananda had no chance to escape. One day the Buddha and his Arhats went out for lunch and left Sundarananda to watch the door. "Today is the day!" thought Sundarananda. "I'm definitely going home."

Before the Buddha left, however, he had instructed Sundarananda to sweep the floor. Eager to be on his way, he went right to work, but every time he got the dust together, a gust of wind blew it all over the room. He tried closing the window, but when he closed one, the other blew open. Strange. This went on for two or three hours. "The Buddha will be back any minute," he thought. "Dust or no dust, I'm leaving!" He threw the broom down and ran.

"The Buddha uses the main road," he thought, "so I'll take to the side road." He ran for a couple of miles when suddenly he saw the Buddha walking toward him. He hid behind a tree to wait for him to pass, moving slowly around the back of the tree so that he would not be seen. Who would have guessed that the Buddha would follow him around the tree, step by step? Sundarananda walked in one direction and the Buddha followed him. Sundarananda reversed his steps and so did the Buddha. A collision was inevitable; there was no place to hide.

"What are you doing?" asked the Buddha. "I thought you were watching the door?"

"I waited and waited," said the embarrassed Sundarananda, "but you didn't return so I came to welcome you. I thought that your bowl might be too heavy... I... I came to help you carry your bowl!"

"Wonderful," said the Buddha. "What a good little brother. Now, let's go back to the Jeta Grove."

The Buddha knew that Sundarananda wasn't happy, and one day he said, "Sundarananda, come with me for a hike in the mountains."

"All right," said Sundarananda thinking, "If I get the chance, I'll surely run away."

The mountains were full of monkeys, five or six hundred of them. "Sundarananda," said the Buddha, "compare these monkeys with your wife. Are they more beautiful than she?"

Sundarananda said, "Why Buddha, of course Sundari is more beautiful. Monkeys are ugly; how can you compare them with Sundari?"

"You're quite intelligent," said the Buddha. "You know that your wife is prettier than the monkeys."

When they had returned to the Jeta Grove, the Buddha said, "Sundarananda, you have never been to the heavens. Want to go?"

"First the mountains, now the heavens. I wonder what they're like?"

Sundarananda and the Buddha sat in meditation and the Buddha used his spiritual powers to take him to the heavens where they visited a palace where five hundred goddesses and many servants were working. The heavens were a million times more beautiful than the world of men, and Sundarananda had never seen such beautiful women. Naturally, he fell in love. "Don't you have a leader?" he asked. "Who is your master?"

"Our master hasn't arrived," they said. "He's Shakyamuni Buddha's little brother, Sundarananda. He's left home to cultivate the Way and in the future he will be reborn with these five hundred goddesses as his wives."

Sundarananda was delighted. "I don't think I'll run away after all," he thought. "I'll cultivate diligently and get reborn in heaven instead."

"Sundarananda," said the Buddha, "are the goddesses more beautiful than Sundari, or is she more beautiful than they?"

"Compared to the goddesses, Sundari is as ugly as a monkey," said Sundarananda.

"Which would you prefer?" said the Buddha.

"The goddesses!" said Sundarananda. "Sundari is beautiful, but the goddesses are out of this world."

"In the future you'll be born here," said the Buddha. "Now let's go back and cultivate."

Sundarananda meditated day and night, cultivating to be a heavenly lord. The Buddha knew that heavenly blessings have outflows, are not ultimate, and that those who enjoy them can still fall to lower realms. Wishing to wake Sundarananda up, he said, "There's nothing going on today. Would you like to visit the hells?"

"I've heard that they aren't very scenic," said Sundarananda, "but if you want to take me there, I'll go."

They visited the hells of the mountain of knives, the sword-tree hell, the fire-sea hell, the ice hell, and many others. Finally, they came to a hell where two ghosts were boiling a pot of oil. The lazy ghosts had let the fire go out and the oil wasn't even simmering. "What are you two doing," said Sundarananda, "fooling around and going to sleep?"

The two ghosts opened their eyes and stared. "What do you care?" they said. "We're in no hurry. We're waiting for someone who isn't due for a long, long time."

"Who?" said Sundarananda.

"Shakyamuni Buddha's little brother, Sundarananda, if you must know," they said. "He left home, but seeks only the blessings of the heavens and the five hundred goddesses. He'll be living in heaven for a thousand years, but in his confusion he will forget how to cultivate and will commit many offenses. This will create evil karma and drag him into the hells to be deep-fried in this very pot."

Every hair on Sundarananda's body stood straight up on end, and every pore ran with cold sweat. "How could this happen to me?" he moaned. From that moment on, he stopped cultivating for rebirth in the heavens and resolved to end birth and death. Soon he certified to Arhatship.

Sundarananda was extremely handsome. The Buddha had the thirty-two marks of a superman and Sundarananda had thirty. Some people even mistook him for the Buddha. One day Shariputra was debating with some non-Buddhists who were even more extreme than many hippies; they didn't wear any clothes at all. "This is our original face," they said. "Why disguise yourself by wearing clothes?"

Shariputra, although not very tall, was extremely intelligent; his replies left them speechless, as if they had no mouths at all. Later, when Sundarananda, who was tall and handsome, happened along, the nudists said, "If that short little Bhikshu beat us, how could we possibly out-talk this tall one?" They bowed to Sundarananda as their teacher and left the home life. Sundarananda had a lot of faithful disciples, and their cultivation was very successful.

This is the story of Sundarananda, who gave up his wife for the goddesses and then, fearing the hells, cultivated the Way.

Ananda

Ananda was the Buddha's cousin. His name means "rejoicing,"[46] and was chosen because he was born on the day the Buddha awoke to the unsurpassed enlightenment. Both his birth and the Buddha's realization were causes for rejoicing.

Of all the great disciples, the Venerable Ananda was foremost in learning. He edited and compiled all the Buddha's sutras, and remembered clearly, without ever forgetting, all the Dharma the Buddha spoke. Ananda's memory was extremely accurate and his samadhi was firm. In fact, Ananda had eight inconceivable states:

1) He never accepted special invitations. In the *Shurangama Sutra* we read that, because he accepted a special lunch invitation, Ananda became involved in an unfortunate encounter with Matangi's daughter. Matangi used a Brahma Heaven mantra to lure

---

46. *qing xi* 慶喜

Ananda into a house of prostitution. Then the Buddha spoke the Shurangama mantra and ordered Manjushri Bodhisattva to take the mantra to rescue him. Ananda never accepted another special invitation. They're too dangerous!

For a member of the Sangha to go out alone to receive offerings from Dharma protecting laymen is called "accepting special invitation," and is against the Buddha's rules. If there are ten Bhikshus, but a layman favors only one with an invitation, he may not go; all ten must go. The Venerable Ananda realized his mistake and never made it again.

2) He never wore the Buddha's old clothes. The Bhikshus liked to wear the Buddha's old clothing. Some even fought over it, feeling that wearing the Buddha's clothes would increase their wisdom and wipe away their offenses. Actually they were just greedy. Ananda never wore them.

3) He did not look at what he should not look at. What he was supposed to see, he looked at; what he was not supposed to see, he avoided. He did not look at what violated the code of morality, but looked only at what was in accord with it.

4) He did not give rise to defiled thoughts. The Venerable Ananda followed the Buddha to the heavens, to the palace of the asuras, and to the palace of the dragons. He saw the heavenly women, the asura women, and the dragon women, the most beautiful women in all of creation, but felt no sexual desire.

5) He knew which samadhi the Buddha had entered. The other Bhikshus didn't know.

6) He knew the benefits received by the beings who were taught and transformed by the Buddha in samadhi.

7) He understood completely all the Dharma the Buddha spoke.

8) He never had to ask to have a Dharma repeated. He remembered it all and never needed to hear one twice.

No one but Ananda had these eight inconceivable states.

Concerning not accepting special invitations, Shramaneras cannot eat or drink when they please, but must eat with the assembly. Novices and Bhikshus alike cannot live with the group and yet eat separately. Even a cup of tea should be taken with the group without assuming a special style. If everyone doesn't receive an apple, an orange, or even a piece of candy, no single person is allowed to eat them on his own.

Rahula

The Buddha's father, King Suddhodana, was afraid that his son the prince would leave the home-life. When the prince was still quite young, his father told him to marry, and he wed Yasodhara. When he was nineteen, he left home and, as he was about to go, his wife told him she wanted a son. The prince thereupon pointed his finger at her, and she became pregnant. Then he left for the Snow Mountains to meditate for six years, and for six years Rahula, his son, lay in his mother's womb.

Rahula means "obstacle."[47] He had plugged up a mousehole for six days in a past life, and so received six years of retribution, suffering in the womb. When he was finally born, he caused a lot of trouble for his mother. King Suddhodana and the whole family were upset. "Well, I never!" they said. "Without a husband, she gives birth to a son. Yasodhara has obviously been running around. She must have a boyfriend."

"She's a bad women," pronounced the entire clan. One servant spoke in her defense. "You're wrong," she said. "She is pure. She stays home all day long and doesn't flirt with men. The child really is the Prince's."

No one believed the servant, and they wanted to kill Yasodhara, to beat her to death. Finally, they dug a pit, built a fire in it, and prepared to throw Yasodhara and her baby in. Yasodhara stepped forward and made a vow. "Heaven spirits! Earth spirits! Bear

---

[47]. *fu zhang* 覆障

witness! If the child belongs to the Prince, my son and I will not be burned. If I did transgress, we both will burn!" Then she jumped into the pit. What do you think happened? The pit turned into a pool of water, and a golden lotus grew out of it to catch them. Everyone then knew that the child was truly the son of the Buddha.

When the Buddha returned to the palace, Yasodhara took Rahula to meet him. If the child had been illegitimate, she certainly would have feared the Buddha. But she sent the child out to meet him and the Buddha hugged the child.

Rahula sought the true Way and worked hard. Among the great disciples he was foremost in secret practices. He worked everywhere, at all times, but no one knew he was working because he never advertised his cultivation. His work was so secret that he could enter samadhi any place at all, even on the toilet, and no one knew.

Although Rahula was the Buddha's son, the Buddha doesn't have only one son; he has Three Kinds of Sons:

1) True Sons. One often reads in the sutras, "...headed by the Dharma Prince Manjushri..." The Buddha is the Dharma King, and the Bodhisattvas are the Buddha's genuine sons.

2) Initiate Sons. These are the Arhats who, out of ignorance, hold to the principle of one-sided emptiness and have not attained the principle of the Middle Way.

3) Uninitiate Sons. Common men who do not know how to cultivate are upside-down, but they are still the Buddha's sons, for the Buddha is the great compassionate father of all living beings. The *Wonderful Dharma Lotus Blossom Sutra* speaks of us as poor, lost sons. We should quickly return to our great compassionate father. We all have a share in the Buddha's family.

Gavampati

This Venerable One's very strange name means "cow cud."[48] Far in the distant past, he had insulted a Bhikshu who couldn't eat hard things and had to slurp his food because his teeth were no good. "You eat like a cow!" said Gavampati. The old Bhikshu happened to be a Pratyeka Buddha, and because of Gavampati's careless slander, Gavampati was reborn for five hundred lifetimes as a cow and got to know the real bitterness that it involved.

Finally he met Shakyamuni Buddha, learned to cultivate, and attained Arhatship. Although he had certified to the fruit, his habits from so many lives remained unchanged, and all day he snorted like a cow chewing its cud. Shakyamuni Buddha was afraid that someone might slander him and reap the same reward, and so he sent the Venerable Gavampati to heaven to live. There he became the foremost of those who receive the offerings of the gods.

We should take care not to speak rashly or to scold others. If you berate others, others will berate you.

Pindola Bharadvaja

Pindola Bharadvaja means "unmoving sharp roots."[49] To the present day he has not entered Nirvana because he broke a rule.

Although the Arhats around the Buddha had spiritual powers, they were not allowed to display them casually. Once an elder called Jyotiska carved a bowl out of sandalwood, put it on top of a high pole, and said, "Whoever can use his spiritual powers to get the bowl down can have it." Pindola Bharadvaja couldn't resist the temptation, and used his powers to get the bowl down.

"Since you're so greedy for sandalwood bowls that you display your spiritual powers," said the Buddha, "you will not be allowed to enter Nirvana. Instead, you must stay here and be a field of blessedness for living beings."

Pindola Bharadvaja is still in the world, but no one knows where. Whenever people make offerings to the Triple Jewel,

---

48. *niu ci* 牛呵
49. *bu dong li ken* 不動利根

however, he comes to receive them, acting as a field of blessedness for beings in the Dharma-ending age.

Kalodayin

Kalodayin means "black light."[50] His skin was black but his body glowed, and his eyes emitted light. One night as he was out walking, a pregnant woman was so startled to see his two bright eyes and black-lit body that she had a miscarriage and died. Because of this the Buddha set up a precept forbidding Shramanas to take walks at night.

Black Light served the Buddha as an attendant and a Dharma Protector. He was the foremost teacher who taught and transformed the greatest number of people, creating over one thousand certified sages.

Mahakapphina

Maha means "great" and *Kapphina* means "constellation."[51] His father and mother prayed to one of the twenty eight constellations in order to have their son. He was foremost in knowledge of astrology.

Vakkula

Vakkula means "good bearing."[52] He was extremely handsome. In the past, during the time of Vipasyin Buddha, he made offerings of the Indian haritaki fruit to a Pratyeka Buddha, a sage enlightened to conditions. Because of this he received the retribution of long life in every life for ninety-one aeons. Foremost of the disciples in age, he lived to be a hundred and sixty.

---

50. *hei guang* 黑光
51. *fang su* 房宿
52. *shan rong* 善容

In past lives, Vakkula kept the precept against killing so conscientiously that he never killed a single creature, not even grass or trees. Thus he obtained "five kinds of death-free retribution."

Vakkula was a strange child. He was not born crying like most children, but entered the world smiling. Not only was he smiling, he was sitting upright in full lotus. Seeing this, his mother exclaimed, "He's a monster!" and threw him on the brazier to burn. After three or four hours, he hadn't burned; he just sat there in full lotus laughing. Fully convinced that he was a monster, she then tried to boil him. When she took the cover off the pot several hours later, he just smiled back at her. "Oh no!" she cried, and threw him into the ocean. He did not drown, however, because a big fish swam up and swallowed him whole. Then a man netted the fist and cut it open. Vakkula stepped out, unharmed by the knife. So the fire didn't burn him, the water didn't boil him, the ocean didn't drown him, the fish didn't chomp him to death, and the fisherman's knife didn't cut him. Because he kept the precept against killing in every life, he obtained these "five kinds of death-free retribution."

Aniruddha

Aniruddha means "not poor."[53] Long ago, during the time of Pusya Buddha, a famine starved the people and reduced them to eating grass, roots, and leaves. It was the practice of a Pratyeka Buddha who lived at that time to go out begging only once every two weeks. If he received no offerings, he simply didn't eat. Once day he went down the mountain to beg and, having received no offerings, was returning with his empty bowl when he was seen by a poor farmer – Aniruddha. The poor farmer addressed the Pratyeka Buddha most respectfully. "Holy Master," he said, "you received no offerings. Won't you please accept my lunch? As I am very poor, I can only offer you this cheap grade of rice, but if you want it, you can have it." Seeing his sincerity, the Pratyeka Buddha

---

[53.] *wu pin* 無貧

accepted. After eating, he ascended into empty space, manifested the eighteen miraculous changes, and left.

Just then the poor farmer saw a rabbit running towards him. The rabbit jumped up on his back, and no matter how the farmer tried to knock, brush, or shake it off, it wouldn't budge. All alone in the field and terrified, he ran home. When he got there the rabbit had turned into a gold statue. He asked his wife to knock the rabbit off, but she couldn't move it either. When they broke a gold leg off the rabbit, another would grow back in its place. In this way, the gold statue was never exhausted, and for ninety-one kalpas Aniruddha was "not poor."

During the time of Shakyamuni Buddha he was the son of the Buddha's father's brother, the Red Rice King. He was the Buddha's first cousin.

Although he wasn't poor, Aniruddha liked to sleep when the Buddha lectured on the sutras. One day the Buddha scolded him:

Hey! Hey! How can you sleep,
Like an oyster or a clam?
Sleep, sleep for a thousand years,
But you'll never hear the Buddha's name!

Hearing this, Aniruddha became extremely vigorous and didn't sleep for seven days. As a consequence, he went blind. The Buddha took pity on him and taught him how to cultivate the "vajra illuminating bright samadhi." He immediately obtained the penetration of the Heavenly Eye; he could see the great trichiliocosm as clearly as seeing an apple held in his hand, and was foremost of the disciples in possessing the Heavenly Eye.

The Assembly Of Bodhisattvas

Sutra:

Together with all the Bodhisattvas, Mahasattvas: Dharma Prince Manjushri, Ajita Bodhisattva, Gandhahastin Bodhisattva, Nityodyukta Bodhisattva, and others such as these, all great Bodhisattvas, and together with Shakra, chief among gods, and the numberless great multitudes from all the heavens.

Commentary:

Not only were the sixteen venerable Arhats present in the assembly, but there were also all the Bodhisattvas, Mahasattvas, the great Bodhisattvas.

What is a Bodhisattva? Bodhisattva is a Sanskrit word. *Bodhi* means "enlightenment" and *sattva* means "being." The word means "to enlighten those with sentience," that is, to cause living beings to wake up.

Bodhisattva also means "enlightened among beings" because Bodhisattvas themselves are awake. Enlightenment is simply the opposite of confusion; confusion is simply non-enlightenment. With one enlightened thought, you are a Buddha. With one confused thought, you are a living being. With every thought enlightened, in every thought you are a Buddha. With every thought confused, in every thought you are a living being.

Bodhisattvas are beings who can wake themselves up. Every day they are more enlightened, not more confused.

Bodhisattvas are enlightened beings and living beings are confused beings. Enlightened beings are those who are enlightened among all the confused living beings. In all situations, they are awake. And so it is said,

> *If you see affairs and are awake,*
> *You can transcend the world.*
> *If you see affairs and are confused,*
> *You fall beneath the wheel.*

Bodhisattvas transcend the world; living beings fall beneath the grinding wheel of sense objects. The difference between Bodhisattvas and living beings is that of enlightenment and confusion. We say, "Enlightened, you're a Buddha." Enlightened, too, you are a Bodhisattva. Confused, you're a living being.

Manjushri

Manjushri, also Sanskrit, means "wonderfully lucky,"[54] or "wonderful virtue."[55] Of the Bodhisattvas, he is foremost in wisdom and is also known as "The Great and Wise Manjushri."

When the Bodhisattva Manjushri was born, ten auspicious signs manifested to indicate that his merit and virtue were complete and his wisdom foremost:

1) The room was filled with bright light. When Manjushri was born, a bright light filled the room. It was not the light of the sun, moon, stars or lamps. It represented Manjushri's great Prajna wisdom and great intelligence which can disperse all darkness.

---

54. *miao ji xiang* 妙吉祥
55. *miao de* 妙德

2) The vessels were filled with sweet dew. Sweet dew[56] is the heavenly medicine of immortality which nourishes you and satisfies your hunger so that you don't need to eat. Sweet dew satisfies, purifies, and refreshes. Hungry ghosts who have sweet dew poured over their heads immediately get rid of their offense karma and obtain a good rebirth. This is called "opening the sweet dew door." When it opens, the hungry ghosts run in and obtain their fill. Sweet dew filling the vessels represents Manjushri's use of the sweet dew of Dharma to rescue living beings.

3) The seven jewels came forth from the earth. When Manjushri was born, gold, silver, lapis lazuli, crystal, mother-of-pearl, red pearls, and carnelian came forth from the earth.

Why are they called "jewels?" Because they are rare. Whatever is scarce is precious. Earth, for example, is actually very precious. Without it we couldn't sustain our lives, and yet no one thinks it is special because there is a lot of it. If you tried to give people a handful of dirt, they wouldn't want it; they'd just throw it away. Water, too, is essential for life, but no one prizes it because it's everywhere. All living things depend on water for survival. Therefore Lao Zi said,

> *"The highest goodness, like water, benefits all things and yet does not contend. It goes to places men despise and so it is close to the Way."*[57]

Water benefits all things, but doesn't struggle. It would never say, "Hey, flower! Fortunately for you there is me, water, and so you have grown so big and bloomed so beautifully. Without me, flower, would this day have come for you? You really should be grateful." It doesn't think in this way and it doesn't wrangle. Travellers will notice that water gathers in the lowlands, in places where men do not like to go. It lives where no one else wants to live and so it is close in its nature to the Way.

---

56. *gan lu* 甘露
57. Lao Zi's *Dao De Jing*, "Classics of the Way and its Virtue."

Water, fire, metal, wood, and earth benefit all things but because of their abundance, no one considers them precious. Trees are everywhere and so no one values them, but gold is a treasure because it is rare. In the Land of Ultimate Bliss, where the ground is made of gold, dirt would be valuable. If you gave a clod of Saha dirt to someone in the Land of Ultimate Bliss... Ah!... it would be as precious as those rocks they are now bringing back from the moon. They are just rocks, but because they came from the moon they are very valuable. If you sent a worthless clod of dirt to the Land of Ultimate Bliss everyone would exclaim, "Rare indeed!" So, the seven precious gems are called "jewels" because they are hard to find.

Manjushri Bodhisattva has limitless treasuries of jewels. When he was born, the seven jewels welled up from the earth – endless for the taking and inexhaustible in their use.

"Where are these treasuries?" you ask.

They are in the place where Manjushri was born.

"Can I go there?"

Don't be so greedy. The travel expenses would cost more than the jewels you'd bring back. So don't have this false thought.

4) The gods opened the treasuries. Wheel-turning Sage Kings[58] have seven treasures: a golden disc, white elephants, jade women, horse, pearls, ministers of the army, and gods to guard his treasuries. These treasuries were buried in the earth long ago and then forgotten, but when Manjushri was born, the guardian gods opened the treasuries so that the jewels could be obtained.

5) Chickens gave birth to phoenixes. Chickens usually give birth to chickens, but when Manjushri was born they gave birth to phoenixes. Phoenixes are auspicious birds, and seeing one is a lucky sign.

---

58. Skt. *cakravarti-raja*

In the *Analects*, Confucius wrote, "The phoenix hasn't come and the river sends no map; I am finished." The phoenix appears when a wise man rules and things are right in the world, as during the time of Emperor Shun (2255 B.C.) when these birds were commonly seen. During the time of Fu Xi (2852 B.C.) a turtle rose out of the river with a chart on its back. The chart gave Fu Xi the idea for the eight trigrams which combine to make the sixty-four hexagrams of the *I Ching*, the Book of Changes. "But now," said Confucius, "one no longer sees such auspicious signs. Thus I know that it's all over. To expound the Way and its virtue is of no use."

6) Pigs gave birth to dragons. Dragons ordinarily give birth to dragons and phoenixes ordinarily give birth to phoenixes. It's not too strange for chickens to hatch phoenixes, but then pigs gave birth to dragons – dragon pigs, with scales.

7) Horses gave birth to unicorns. Horses usually beget horses, but they had unicorns. Unicorns, lions, and tigers are all called the "kings of beasts."

The unicorn is also an auspicious animal. In China, during the time of the benevolent Emperor Tang Di Yao (2356 B.C.), there were many phoenixes and unicorns, and they were often seen. Later, when people's karmic retribution grew too heavy, these auspicious creatures no longer appeared. Confucius wrote,

> *In the time of Emperor Tang Yao*
> *the unicorn and phoenix abounded.*
> *That time, however, is not the present,*
> *so what have you come to seek?*
> *Unicorn! Unicorn! How my heart grieves…*

"During the time of Emperor Tang Yao, unicorns and phoenixes often came into the world to roam around; everyone saw them. But that time is not now, so what have you come to seek?" he said.

When the Sage Confucius was born, a unicorn appeared. When his mother saw it, she tied a string around its neck. Near the end of

Confucius' life, some hunters killed a unicorn. When Confucius saw it, he noticed that it had the string around its neck; it was the same unicorn. Seeing this sign, he sighed deeply, for he knew that it would not be long before he died. "Unicorn! Unicorn! How my heart grieves..." he said.

When Manjushri was born, horses gave birth to unicorns.

8) Cows gave birth to white *zai*. The white zai is an extremely rare and auspicious animal. It's not like an ox and it's not like a horse; it's not like a deer or a mule. It's not like anything at all. It looks like a horse, but has the hooves of an ox.

9) The grain in the granaries turned to gold. What use is golden grain? Can you eat it?

"You can exchange it for money and buy a lot of grain," you may say.

I agree. A grain of gold is very valuable.

10) Elephants with six tusks appeared. Elephants usually have only two tusks, but when Manjushri was born they had six.

These are the ten auspicious signs which appeared at Manjushri's birth. They represent the Ten Paramitas: giving, morality, patience, vigor, concentration, wisdom, skill in means, vows, determination, and knowledge. They show that Manjushri is not like other Bodhisattvas.

If you would like to meet Manjushri Bodhisattva, you must first remember these ten signs. Then when you see him you will know, "This is my old friend and closest good knowing advisor."

Manjushri will be very pleased. "Yes! You are my old friend, my very good friend," he will say. Although he doesn't discriminate, if you don't know him, he won't approach you. The better you know him, the closer he comes. Therefore we should know the states of the Bodhisattvas so that we can be their brothers and friends. All the Bodhisattvas are our good knowing advisors, and in the future we will be Bodhisattvas, too. So don't take yourselves lightly.

Ajita

Ajita is Sanskrit for "invincible."[59] Ajita Bodhisattva is none
other than Maitreya, "compassionate clan,"[60] Bodhisattva. He
specializes in cultivating the "compassionate heart samadhi" and is
compassionate toward all living beings. Scolded, beaten, cheated,
insulted, no matter how badly he is treated, he is compassionate in
return. No matter how obnoxious living beings are, he protects
them all even more lovingly than he would protect his own sons or
daughters. His compassion and loving concern are limitless and
boundless.

In order to cultivate the compassionate heart samadhi, you must
first practice patience, and so Ajita Bodhisattva wrote this verse:

> *The Old Fool wrapped in ragged clothes,*
> *His belly filled with gruel,*
> *He mends old sacks to keep him warm*
> *And lives on chance, Old Fool.*
> *A scolding makes the Fool smile sweetly,*
> *While a beating makes him sleepy;*
> *Spit on his face, he lets it dry*
> *And saves his strength and energy.*
> *His calm, a peace past ridicule*
> *Gets him the jewel within the wonderful;*
> *Now that you've heard this song today*
> *Why worry about not perfecting the Way?*

The song is about a stupid old man who wears a patched robe
and eats his food plain, without soy sauce, hot sauce, or sesame oil.
It doesn't taste like much, but it fills his stomach. He mends his
robes to stay warm and whatever happens, just happens:

---

59. *wu neng sheng* 無能勝
60. *ci shi* 慈氏

Something happens and he reflects it;
When it passes, he is still.

Everywhere according with conditions
  as the years and months go by;
Minding your own business
  as the time passes.

When it happens, it happens; when it's over, it's gone. He accords with conditions and does not change, does not change and yet accords with conditions. For him,

In movement, there is stillness,
In stillness, movement;
Both movement and stillness
Are still and moving.

But we won't speak about it too deeply. If we did, it would be difficult to understand.

Scolded, the Old Fool says, "Great!" If someone hits him, he falls asleep. Now isn't that stupid? If ordinary people were hit, they would glare and shout, "Why did you hit me!" But the Old Fool just falls asleep. Isn't this wonderful? If you can master this, you're doing pretty well; you have truly gained some genuine cultivation.

"Spit in my face," says the stupid old man, "and I just let it dry." If you spit in someone else's face, the fire of ignorance would blaze thirty thousand feet into the air. "How can you insult me like that?" he'd say. But the old man doesn't even wipe if off. He just lets it dry. Although it's not much effort to wipe it away, he still saves his strength and gives others no affliction.

This is *paramita.* If you can sleep when people hit you and let their spit dry on your face, this is *ksanti-paramita,* the perfection of patience. If you do not understand this, what Buddhadharma do you study? You study day in and day out, but when this happens, you don't know what dharma it is. If someone hit you to test your skill, you'd probably end up saying, "I've studied the Buddhadharma for so long. Why can't I use it when the time comes?"

The paramita is the wonderful within the wonderful, the jewel within the jewel. If you've heard this news, how can you worry about not perfecting the Way? The Buddhas and Bodhisattvas would never deceive you.

This, then, is what Ajita Bodhisattva had to say about the perfection of patience, and if we practice accordingly we shall certainly realize the Way.

Gandhahastin and Nityodyukta

Gandhahastin is a Sanskrit word which is interpreted as "never resting."[61] *Nityodyukta*, also Sanskrit, means "ever-vigorous."[62] "Ever-vigorous" and "Never-resting" competed with each other. One was vigorous and the other never rested; one never rested and the other was vigorous. They watched each other: "If you don't rest," said one, "then I'll be constantly vigorous."

"If you're ever vigorous," replied the other, "then I won't rest." In the six periods of the day and night they practiced the Way, each acting as the other's Dharma protector. They raced every step of the way, and neither would let himself fall behind. Thus Gandhahastin is just Nityodyukta; Ever-vigorous is just Never-resting.

These two have cultivated together as Dharma friends for limitless kalpas. "If you work hard, I'll work harder! If you increase your efforts, I'll double mine." They are genuine cultivators, ever-vigorous and never-resting, Nityodyukta and Gandhahastin.

---

61. *bu xiu xi* 不休息
62. *chang jing jin* 常精進

Shakra, and the multitudes from heavens

Shakra, chief among gods, and the numberless great multitudes from all the heavens. Shakra, or Sakro Devanam Indra, is the ruler of the Trayastrimsa Heaven, the Heaven of the Thirty-three. He is referred to in the Shurangama mantra as *Yin Tuo La Ye*. Those who understand the Buddhadharma know that all gods, ghosts, and spirit kings, as well as all the great Bodhisattvas are contained within the Shurangama mantra. Those who do not understand the Buddhadharma say, "Buddhism does not include the heavens, the twenty-eight constellations..." They say this because they don't understand that the heavens and the constellations, everything is within the Shurangama mantra. Shakra is Sanskrit; it means "the able heavenly ruler."[63]

Numberless great multitudes from all the heavens. Numberless, the heavens cannot be counted. In general there are thirty-three, but if you were to describe them in detail, you would speak of the limitless heavens within each heaven, just as there are also limitless worlds within each world and limitless countries within each country. Thus, many heavenly beings were present in the assembly.

[63.] *neng tian zhu* 能天主

PART IV

THE PRINCIPLE PROPER

Sutra:

At that time the Buddha told the Elder Shariputra, "Passing from here through hundreds of thousands of millions of Buddhalands to the West, there is a world called Ultimate Bliss. In this land a Buddha called Amitabha right now teaches the Dharma.

Commentary:

At that time refers to the time when all the gods, Bodhisattvas, Sravakas, Bhiksus, Bhiksunis, Upasakas, and Upasikas had gathered together to listen to Shakyamuni Buddha. The Buddha spoke to the wise elder Shariputra saying, "If you travel westward from here, from the pure abode in the Jeta Grove in the Garden of the Benefactor of Orphans and the Solitary, Sravasti, India, and go through hundreds of thousands of millions of Buddhalands, you will find a world system called 'the Land of Ultimate Bliss.' This is the happiest land there is. Nothing surpasses the happiness there, it is ultimate.

"In this land, there is a Buddha. His name is *Amitabha*, 'limitless light.' He is also called *Amitayus*, 'limitless life.' His light is measureless, illumining the lands of the ten directions everywhere without obstruction, and his lifespan extends for hundreds of thousands of tens of thousands of millions of great kalpas without end." After realising Buddhahood, this Buddha did not rest, but right now he speaks the Dharma. He is not an unemployed Buddha; teaching the Dharma is the Buddha's job. Whoever teaches the Dharma does the Buddha's work; whoever doesn't, does the demons' work. So it is said,

> *"Unless I teach the Dharma to save living beings, I will have passed through my entire life in vain."*

If you don't teach the Dharma and convert living beings, you will have wasted your life and obtained no benefit.

Sutra:

"Shariputra, for what reason is this land called Ultimate Bliss?

Commentary:

"Shariputra!" said the Buddha, "Why is this land called Ultimate Bliss?"

Although he had great wisdom, Shariputra didn't know enough to ask this question, and so the Buddha asked it himself. This is like yesterday when I asked you if you had any questions and you didn't answer because you didn't know what to ask. So I said, "Very well, I have a question for you. Do you like the rain?"

Thieves hate the rain. Why? If they go out to steal, they get all wet. "I want to steal something," they say, "but it is raining. I will have to carry an umbrella. How inconvenient!"

Travellers say, "I came here for a vacation and I haven't seen a thing. Detestable rain!" Travellers and thieves don't care for the rain.

But the farmer says, "Rain! My flowers will sell for thousands of dollars. Isn't this fine?" The fruit growers say, "The rain will make my apples big, fat, and sweet – my oranges too."

Now, would you say that lecturing sutras and speaking about the Dharma is a good thing or not? Those who believe in the Buddhadharma say it is good, but those who are jealous of it say it is not.

Why is this land called Ultimate Bliss? Basically, Shariputra should have asked this question, but he didn't, and so Shakyamuni Buddha said, "Shariputra, why is Amitabha's country called Ultimate Bliss? Speak up!"

The Buddha waited about five minutes. Shariputra said nothing; such great wisdom and yet he didn't know what to say! He just stared blankly as you do when I ask you a question. But time is precious. Shakyamuni Buddha waited until he could wait no more. "All right," he said, "I will answer it myself."

Sutra:

"All living beings of this country endure none of the sufferings, but enjoy every bliss. Therefore it is called 'Ultimate Bliss.'

Commentary:

In Amitabha Buddha's land, living beings are born by transformation from lotus flowers. Their birth is pure, not one of desire and emotions, and so their bodies are pure and are not the result of sexual desire and the lustful thoughts of men and women. This is why they **endure none of the sufferings, but enjoy every bliss**. Why do we suffer? We suffer because our bodies are created from unclean substances of the father's semen and the mother's blood. We continually think of unclean things. Men usually think of women, women of men. People eat their fill and, since there's nothing else to do, sexual desire is foremost. When the time comes, men and women want to marry. If they don't, they feel as if they have a great illness which has not been cured. Because the basis, the seed, is impure, the thoughts are impure, and those impure thoughts bring about all kinds of suffering. Why is there suffering? For no reason other than this.

Sutras are lectured and Dharma is taught only to teach you one thing, have no unclean, impure thoughts, have no sexual desire. Without sexual desire you are one of the clear, pure, ocean-wide assembly of Bodhisattvas. With sexual desire, you are a ghostly living being of the five turbid realms. Cultivation and non-cultivation are right here. If you can purify your mind, your merit and virtue are limitless. If you cannot purify your mind, your offences are limitless. Offences are created from impure thoughts. Such thoughts are causes planted in your self-nature and they result in the manifestation of offences and evil. But if your self-nature is pure, outwardly there will be no evil karmic retribution.

Therefore, you may study the Buddhadharma for several tens of thousands of great kalpas, but unless you understand the genuine doctrine you won't get off the revolving wheel. If you understand the essential message of the Buddhadharma, however, you will know, "Oh! It is simply a matter of purifying my mind and will."

The Buddhadharma teaches you to purify your mind and will. If you understand the Buddhadharma you can become enlightened, and once enlightened, you will never have unclean thoughts again. Why do people suffer? It is because of unclean thoughts. Why is there no suffering in the Land of Ultimate Bliss? It is because the people there have no impure thoughts. Thus, they endure **none of the sufferings, but enjoy every bliss**.

As we recite "Namo Amitabha Buddha" we each create and adorn our own Land of Ultimate Bliss. We each accomplish our own Land of Ultimate Bliss which is certainly not hundreds of thousands of millions of Buddhalands from here. Although it is far away, it doesn't go beyond one thought. It is not hundreds of thousands of millions of Buddhalands from here; it is right in our hearts. The Land of Ultimate Bliss is the original true heart, the true mind, of everyone of us. If you obtain this heart, you will be born in the Land of Ultimate Bliss. If you don't understand your own original true heart, you will not. The Land of Ultimate Bliss is within our hearts, not outside. This land is clear, pure, and undefiled and so is that one thought of the mind and nature. It is just that now, as common people, we are defiled by attachment. If you can empty yourself of attachments, you will immediately see Amitabha Buddha; that is the Land of Ultimate Bliss. Amitabha Buddha and living beings – do not discriminate between this and that, for the Land of Ultimate Bliss is not so far away. In one thought, turn the light within. Know that originally you are the Buddha, and your original Buddhahood is just the Land of Ultimate Bliss.

For this reason, you should cast out your defiled thoughts, your lustful desires, your confusion, jealousy, contrariness, and selfish thoughts of personal gain. Be like the Bodhisattvas who benefit everyone and enlighten all beings. Just that is the Land of Ultimate Bliss. Don't you agree that the absence of confusion and false thoughts is the Land of Ultimate Bliss? If it isn't, what is?

Good knowing advisors, you are all ones of great wisdom and great intelligence. You are all more clever than I, and in the future you will explain the Dharma better than I do. But now, because you don't know Chinese, I am introducing you to this old-fashioned tradition. In the future you will transform it and make it unspeakably wonderful.

Sutra:

"Moreover, Shariputra, this Land of Ultimate Bliss is everywhere surrounded by seven tiers of railings, seven layers of netting, and seven rows of trees, all formed from the four treasures and for this reason named 'Ultimate Bliss.'

Commentary:

After explaining why this land is called Ultimate Bliss, Shakyamuni Buddha waited for Shariputra to ask about the limitless principles which remained but, as intelligent as he was, Shariputra simply didn't know enough to ask. Why? It was because the Pure Land Dharma Door is simply too wonderful.

Unable to wait any longer, the Buddha said, "Shariputra, I will tell you something else. In the most happy land there are seven railings which run horizontally like fences and are arranged vertically in seven tiers." The **railings** represent the precepts, the **netting** represents concentration, and the **trees** represent wisdom. The number **seven** is used for the "Seven Classes," the classification of the Thirty-Seven Wings of Enlightenment into seven groups:

1. The Four Applications of Mindfulness
2. The Four Right Efforts
3. The Four Bases of Supernatural Power
4. The Five Roots
5. The Five Powers
6. The Seven Limbs of Enlightenment
7. The Proper Eight-fold Path

How do the tiers of railings represent the precepts? Precepts prohibit evil and prevent error. Morality is simply

All evil not done and
All good conduct respectfully practised.

Once you have taken the precepts, you cannot entertain confused false thinking. You must purify your mind and will. If you find yourself caught up in false thinking, rub your head and say, "I have left the home-life, I am hairless. I am no longer a layman and so I can't be casual and think unclean thoughts. I must stop." In this way the precepts are like a fence. It is illegal to jump it, you have to go through the gate. Thus, the seven tiers of railings represent the precepts.

How do the seven layers of netting represent concentration? One does not enter or emerge from true concentration. With "naga concentration" you don't need to meditate because no external state will move your heart. You are always concentrated.

Suppose you see something good to eat and think, "Not bad. I will try it out." This displays a lack of concentration power, to say nothing of stealing food, which is a violation of the precepts!

"Oh, a little thing like that is not important," you think.

It's just because you transgress in minor ways, that, when something major comes along you slip up. People who transgress in little matters will transgress even more easily in big ones. It may be a small matter, but it is just the small matters which are difficult to change. If you change your small faults, you have concentration power. Always in concentration,

> *The eyes see forms outside,*
> *but inside there is nothing;*
> *The ears hear external sounds,*
> *but the mind does not know.*

Concentration is the state of being unmoved by situations. For example, when a woman sees a handsome man but has no thought of sexual desire, she is said to possess concentration power. When a man sees a beautiful woman but has no thoughts of sexual desire, that, too, is concentration. Seeing as if not seeing and hearing as if not hearing,

> *The eyes see forms outside,*
> *but inside there is nothing;*
> *The ears hear external sounds,*
> *but the mind does not know.*

The seven layers of netting represent concentration. Now do you understand the *Amitabha Sutra*? If you don't understand it completely, perhaps you understand a little. That's why I am explaining it.

And seven rows of very tall **trees.** The trees represent wisdom. If you have wisdom, you are tall, without it, you are short. It's not a question of how tall or short your body is. With wisdom you are like seven rows of tall trees; without wisdom you are like seven rows of grass! The grass has smothered your heart and you grow more and more stupid.

All formed from the four treasures and for this reason called 'Ultimate Bliss.' The four treasures are gold, silver, lapis lazuli and crystal.

"Is the Land of Ultimate Bliss made out of only four treasures?" You may wonder.

The treasures in the Land of Ultimate Bliss are limitless and measureless, nothing in this world compares with them. We of this world have never seen anything like the treasures which fill that land.

"Then why do you only mention four?" You ask.

The four treasures represent the Four Virtues of Nirvana: permanence, bliss, true self, and purity.

1. Permanence. Amitabha Buddha's lifespan is limitless. Not only does Amitabha Buddha have a limitless lifespan, but when we are born in the Land of Ultimate Bliss, we will, too. If you would like to transcend death, seek rebirth in the Pure Land, because everyone there has limitless life. This is the virtue of permanence.

2. Bliss. Those born in the Pure Land endure none of the sufferings, but enjoy every bliss.

3. True self. In this land, the self has eight great freedoms, eight functions, eight kinds of strength, and eight spiritual penetrations. These are the eight kinds of wonderful function and are called the Eight Great Freedoms of the Self:

a) One body can manifest limitless bodies. If a hundred people invite you to lunch, you can accept all their invitations and go to every Dharma protector's house to eat. One Dharma protector might say, "He came to lunch at my house on such and such a day," and another will say, "but he also had lunch at my house on that day!" They don't know that you are able to respond to limitless offerings in a single day.

b) One body the size of a dust mote can completely fill the great thousand world systems. Isn't this wonderful? In one mote of dust, Buddha-fields appear; in a Buddha-field, motes of dust appear. One country becomes as small as a mote of dust and one mote of dust becomes as large as a country.

c) The great body can lightly float to a distant place. It can fly. The body is big and awkward, yet it can gently float far away.

d) One manifests limitless kinds of living beings which always dwell together in one land. We see mountains as mountains when actually they contain the palaces of the Buddhas and Bodhisattvas. You see mountains and oceans but do not see the Buddhas and Bodhisattvas within them who are teaching the Dharma. A layman has mentioned such a place where there are many people cultivating the Way; he can see it and you can't. This is to cause limitless kinds of living beings to dwell in one place.

e) All the organs are used interchangeably. The eyes can speak; the ears can see; the nose can eat. How can this happen? The six sense organs, the eyes, ears, nose, tongue, body and mind are interchangeable. Each of them has the function of the other six. Sages who have given proof to the fruit may speak with Bodhisattvas, but you wouldn't know it if they were talking with their ears!

"I don't believe it," you say.

Of course you don't. If you did, you did have this talent yourself. But because you don't believe, you don't have it. How can you obtain that in which you do not even believe?

f) The suchness of all dharmas without the thought of dharmas is obtained. Although one who realised true self obtains all dharmas, he has no thought of attainment. This is mentioned in the *Heart Sutra* as "no wisdom and no attainment."

g) The meaning of one verse may be explained throughout limitless aeons. The meaning of a single line, a single word, cannot be fully explained even in limitless aeons. Why? Because he has free and unobstructed eloquence so that speaking in any place or in any dimension he always rests in the Way and speaks the Dharma. Speaking Dharma in Buddha-fields and in motes of dust, any dharma he selects contains limitless meanings. Having rightly attained the Eight Great Freedoms, he does what he pleases and says what he likes. He can scold people, but they like to hear it. "He scolds very well," they say. He may teach Dharma by doing nothing but scolding people, and yet they say it is very nice to hear. Why? Because he has attained the Eight Great Freedoms of the Self. Because he himself is free, when you hear him speak, you too, feel free.

h) The body pervades all places, like space. One body fills Buddha-fields in number as many as dust motes, but, like empty space, there is really nothing there. Although there is nothing there, it fills Buddha-fields in number as many as dust motes. What doctrine is this? That of freedom, the Eight Great Freedoms of the Self.

The sutra text below says, "...and throughout the clear morning each living being of that land, with sacks full of the myriads of wonderful flowers, makes offerings to the hundreds of thousands of millions of Buddhas of the other directions. At mealtime they return to their own country and having eaten they stroll around." They can do this because they have obtained the Eight Great Freedoms of the Self.

4. Purity. The last of the four virtues of Nirvana is that of purity. This land is pure. It is adorned with the four treasures which represent the four virtues of Nirvana in unobstructed interpenetration. Thus it is named "Ultimate Bliss."

Sutra:

"Moreover, Shariputra, this Land of Ultimate Bliss has pools of the seven jewels, filled with the waters of eight meritorious virtues. The bottom of each pool is pure, spread over with golden sand. On the four sides are stairs of gold, silver, lapis lazuli, and crystal; above are raised pavilions

adorned with gold, silver, lapis lazuli, crystal, mother-of-pearl, red pearls, and carnelian.

"In the pools are lotuses as large as carriage wheels, green colored of green light, yellow colored of yellow light, red colored of red light, white colored of white light, subtly, wonderfully, fragrant and pure.

"Shariputra, the realisation of the Land of Ultimate Bliss is thus meritoriously adorned.

Commentary:

The previous passage of text described the exquisite beauty of the Land of Ultimate Bliss. This passage praises the subtle wonder of its water-pools. Having spoken of the seven rows of trees, the seven layers of netting, and the seven tiers of railing, Shakyamuni Buddha was waiting for Shariputra to ask further about that land. But the great, wise Shariputra, the Buddha's most intelligent disciple, still did not know where to begin and probably hesitated for several minutes until the Buddha himself said, "**Moreover, Shariputra, this Land of Ultimate Bliss has pools of the seven jewels.**" There are pools in the Saha world, but they are made of mud or cement. No one makes pools out of gold, silver, lapis lazuli, crystal, mother-of-pearl, red pearls, or carnelian.

Lapis lazuli is an opaque, blue semi-precious stone. It could be found near the country of Magadha, in central India. **Crystal** is also called "water jade." **Mother-of-pearl** has what looks like cart tracks running across it. Translated from the Chinese it is "great shells."

The pools were not man-made. On the contrary, they appeared naturally. Within the pools, one finds the **waters of eight meritorious virtues**:

1. Tepid. It is warm and yet it is cool. In other words, once you get in the pool, if you want it a little warmer, it becomes so. If you think, "It is too hot. A little cooler, please," then it becomes cooler. The quality of the water is inconceivable.

2. Pure. No matter how many times you wash with this water, it doesn't get dirty. Unlike the water in our world, the more you wash with the water of the Land of Ultimate Bliss, the cleaner it gets. It feels like milk running over your body, smooth, comfortable, and extremely fine and subtle to the touch. The more you wash with it, the nicer you feel, there is no better feeling than this.

3. Sweet. You don't have to drink it. Just wash with it, and you will know that it is very, very sweet. My disciple She Guo Man in Hong Kong came to Guan Yin cave where I was living once and ate noodles and drank water from my pool. Then she said, "Ah! This water is so sweet! Does it have sugar in it?"

"No," I replied, "It is just plain water."

"But it is so sweet!" she said.

"Perhaps Guan Yin Bodhisattva has given you some sweet dew," I said.

"Oh!" she exclaimed, and was really delighted. At that time I was wearing rags and you could see my flesh through the holes in them. What do you think she did? She made me two sets of clothes, because she liked the sweet water. The water in the Land of Ultimate Bliss is also sweet and delicious.

4. Soft. The water is not hard. It is very light and soft.

5. Moistening. When dirty people wash with it, they become clean. This water will wash any filth right off your body and leave you bright and clean.

6. Harmonising. If you wash with his water, your heart and mind will be at peace, without the slightest trace of bad temper. Without a hot temper, without the fire of ignorance, and without affliction, you will be in harmony with everyone. If they scold you, you won't get angry, and if they knock you over, it won't create a problem. "So what if they hit me?" you will say. You will be at peace with everyone. See how fine this is?

7. Banishes hunger and thirst. This is most important. After bathing in the waters of eight meritorious virtues, when it's time to eat, you are not hungry, and when it is time to drink, you are not thirsty. No milk and no bread and yet no hunger or thirst. The Land of Ultimate Bliss is unspeakably wonderful.

8. Nourishes all roots. It gives sustenance to all your sense organs. Your eyes become bright and light and your ears, if once deaf, now can hear. If your nose is stopped up, wash with the water of eight meritorious virtues and it will get to work again. Whatever you eat tastes good, and your hands and feet work without feeling tired. Not only that, the water also nourishes your good roots and gets rid of your bad karma. How great would you say this merit and virtue is? We should quickly seek rebirth in the Land of Ultimate Bliss so that we may bathe in the pools of the waters of eight meritorious virtues, and have our good roots nourished.

This has been a general explanation of the waters of eight meritorious virtues. Were I to speak in detail, I wouldn't finish by the end of a great aeon. These waters have eight independent merits and virtues, eight happy merits and virtues, eight subtle, wonderful, inconceivable merits and virtues, and more. No matter what karmic obstacles you have, they all dissolve when you get into these pools. What are karmic obstacles? They are those things which you dislike, the things which cause you to become afflicted. Without karmic obstacles there is no affliction and this is like a covering of golden sand. When we go to the Land of Ultimate Bliss, the pools of the seven jewels melt away our karmic obstacles.

On the four sides are stairs of gold, silver, lapis lazuli, and crystal. We may think our stairways of marble are splendid, but those in the Land of Ultimate Bliss are inlaid with gold, silver, lapis lazuli, and crystal, and the pathways emit multicolored rays of light.

Above are raised pavilions adorned with gold, silver, lapis lazuli, crystal, mother-of-pearl, red pearls and carnelian. Why are they adorned with so many treasures? To make them beautiful to look at! The seven jewels used to adorn the pavilions represent the perfection of Amitabha Buddha's ten thousand virtues. The great adornments are the measure of his great virtuous practices, for without virtuous practice, there can be no seven jewelled adornments.

In the pools are lotuses as large as carriage wheel. Then how big are the pools? Each is as big as a hundred great seas. One great sea is big indeed, how big would you say a hundred great seas are?

The lotuses in these pools are as large as carriage wheels, which are much bigger than automobile tires. The carriage wheels on the chariot of the Wheel-turning Sage King are one *yojana* in diameter. A small yojana is forty miles, a middle-sized one is sixty miles, and a large one is eighty miles. This lotus, then, is eighty miles in diameter. Lotuses growing in pools as large as a hundred great seas would have to be at least that big. Tiny flowers in such big pools wouldn't look right.

A song about Amitabha Buddha goes like this;

> *Amita, the great sage and master,*
> *Serene, subtle, wonderful, beyond all others...*
>
> *Pools of seven gems,*
> *Flowers of four colors and waves of solid gold.*

Amitabha Buddha is the great sage and master. His countenance is sedate, serene, and very wonderful. There is no image as fine as that of Amitabha Buddha.

The flowers in the pools are **green colored of green light, yellow colored of yellow light, red colored of red light, white colored of white light**. Light, bright light – **subtly, wonderfully, fragrant and pure**. The water is subtle and soft. It looks like water, but when you reach out to touch it, it feels as if nothing were there. It feels like water, but it is so fine that you can't grab a hold of it. It is like there's nothing there, but still it is there. It is just that subtle.

"Wonderful" means ineffable. There is no way you can even think about it. The water is also fragrant. Once you get in it you won't want to get out. As soon as you smell its fragrance, you will bring forth the Bodhi mind. In this world, we chase after good smells, but in the Land of Ultimate Bliss, the fragrances cause one to say, "Too fine! I did better hurry up and cultivate the Way."

The smells of this world cause you to think, "Not bad… it is really bitter at the Temple. Cultivation isn't as good as…" But smells are defiled dharmas. Forms, sounds, smells, tastes and tangible objects are the five sense objects, and cultivators of the Way must certainly see through and break all attachment to them. First of all, do not become attached to beautiful form. Beauty is only skip deep; beneath the skin there is just pus, blood, and flesh. In the *Shurangama Sutra* we read of Matangi's daughter, who couldn't give up her love for Ananda. The Buddha asked her, "What is it about Ananda that you love?"

"I love his eyes," she said.

"All right," said the Buddha, "I will pluck out his eyes and you may have them."

"Oh no," she said. "If you do that, they won't be of any use."

"If they are of no use, then what are you doing loving them?" asked Shakyamuni Buddha. Hearing this, she immediately certified to the fruit of Arhatship.

So you should not become attached to forms. In order to cultivate, you should borrow forms and sounds and yet not become attached to them. Don't say, "Ah, this music is so beautiful. When I hear it, I… get all confused and don't know what I am doing." If you must sing, sing in praise of Amitabha Buddha. Don't become attached to smells either.

When I was in Hong Kong people used to follow me around. They said I smelled good. I really disliked this and so I put some smelly stuff on myself to keep them away. Everything is made from the mind alone. If you have samadhi power, then fragrances aren't fragrant and bad smells don't stink; good sounds aren't good sounds, and bad sounds aren't bad; beauty isn't beautiful, and ugliness isn't ugly. Samadhi power is the skill one derives from cultivation. If you have this skill, when people are good to you, you are not happy and when they are bad, you don't become afflicted. With samadhi power, you won't listen to the talk of your tongue when it says to you, "Take a taste of this and see if it tastes better than..." I often tell you that when I eat, I don't know if the food is good or not. It is not that I don't *know*. If I didn't know I would be like wood or stone. I am just not affected by the taste. I eat the same amount, whether it tastes good or not, without discrimination.

In the same way, greed for the objects of touch indicates a lack of samadhi power and shows that one has been turned by external states.

The lotuses of four colors in the Land of Ultimate Bliss shine with four colors of light which represent the Four Applications of Mindfulness, the Four Right Efforts, and the Four Bases of Supernatural Power. In reciting and studying the *Amitabha Sutra*, we should cultivate samadhi power. If you have samadhi power, then the Land of Ultimate Bliss is right here. If you don't, even if you went to the Land of Ultimate Bliss, you would run right off to the Land of Ultimate Misery. With samadhi power, the Land of Ultimate Misery is the Land of Ultimate Bliss. Without affliction, you can say, "Everything is okay." If that is not the Land of Ultimate Bliss, what is?

Sutra:

"Moreover, Shariputra, in that Buddhaland there is always heavenly music and the ground is yellow gold. In the six periods of the day and night a heavenly rain of mandarava flowers falls, and throughout the clear morning, each living being of that land, with sacks full of the myriads of wonderful flowers, makes offerings to the hundreds of thousands of millions of Buddhas of the other directions. At

mealtime they return to their own country, and having eaten, they stroll around.

"Shariputra, the realisation of the Land of Ultimate Bliss is thus meritoriously adorned.

Commentary:

Shakyamuni Buddha told Shariputra, "In Amitabha's country, the gods play music all day and all night," throughout the **six periods**: the beginning of the day, the middle of the day, the end of the day, the beginning of the night, the middle of the night, and the end of the night. **Mandarava**, a Sanskrit word, may be interpreted as, "according to your wish,"[64] or "white flower"[65]. However you would like them to be, that's the way these flowers are.

At dawn when the sun is just rising, the living beings of this land, **with sacks full of the myriads of wonderful flowers, make offering to the hundreds of thousands of millions of Buddhas of the other directions**. How long does it take? Not long, just the time it takes to eat a meal, half and hour or so. These living beings can travel to billions of Buddhalands in a very short space of time because they have obtained the Eight Great Freedoms of the Self; they are free and independent, and everything accords with their wishes. Having obtained the "as you will" spiritual penetrations, if they want to go somewhere, they arrive there immediately.

When we bow to the Buddha, we should envision our bodies filling the limitless Buddhalands of the ten directions, personally bowing to all the Buddhas. If you can contemplate the Dharma realm in this way, then your body is as big as the Dharma realm. The *Avatamsaka Sutra* says,

> *"If one wishes to understand completely*
> *The Buddhas of the three periods of time,*

---

[64]. *shi yi hua* 適意華
[65]. *bai hua* 白華

> *He should contemplate the nature of the Dharma realm:*
> *Everything is made from the mind alone.*"

At mealtime they return to the Land of Ultimate Bliss and **having eaten**, they go for a walk.

Sutra:

"**Moreover Shariputra, in this country there are always rare and wonderful vari-colored birds: white cranes, peacocks, parrots, and egret, kalavinkas, and two-headed birds. In the six periods of the day and night the flocks of birds sing forth harmonious and elegant sounds; their clear and joyful sounds proclaim the five roots, the five powers, the seven bodhi shares, the eight sagely way shares, and dharmas such as these. When living beings of this land hear these sounds, they are altogether mindful of the Buddha, mindful of the Dharma, and mindful of the Sangha.**

Commentary:

Since Shariputra still had no questions, Shakyamuni Buddha said "I will tell you a little more, Shariputra. In the Land of Ultimate Bliss there are many kinds of multi-colored birds." They are most unusual and beautiful. **White cranes** are found in our world, too. **Peacocks** are especially beautiful. **Parrots** can talk! They may see you and say, "Hello!" Some Chinese parrots say, "A guest is coming, a guest is coming." Some people even teach their parrots to recite the Buddha's name so that they can be born in the Land of Ultimate Bliss. **Egrets** are the kind of bird after which Shariputra's mother was named. They are also very beautiful.

Kalavinka is a Sanskrit word which means "good sounding bird."[66] Before it has even hatched from its egg, it sings more melodiously than any other bird. **Two-headed birds**[67] have two

---

66. *miao sheng niao* 妙聲鳥
67. *gong ming niao* 共命鳥

heads on one body. Have you ever seen such a bird? Living beings are born this way as karmic retribution for too much sexual activity. Because the husband's and wife's sexual desire was so heavy that they indulged in intercourse day and night, they fell and turned into a bird-body with two heads. They have different consciousness, but the same karmic retribution. So be careful! If your sexual desire is too intense you may become a two-headed bird.

Someone says, "I did like very much to become one of those birds. People would watch over me and feed me and take care of me."

Perhaps. But the birds are animals just the same, and when their lives are over, they fall into the hells. It is dangerous. Don't think that being a bird is a lot of fun, even though they can fly when they want to fly and perch when they want to perch. A bird's retribution is incredible; it's wisdom decreases life after life. But if you have wisdom, you won't fall.

In the **six periods of the day and night**, these birds **sing forth harmonious and elegant sounds**, like a chorale, very fine music. The birds in the Land of Ultimate Bliss are not born as a result of their karmic offences; they are manifestations of Amitabha Buddha's merit and virtue. In the Land of Ultimate Bliss, the three evil ways of rebirth do not exist.

"If there are no animals," you may ask, "then where did all the birds come from?".

They are manifestations of Amitabha Buddha's merit and virtue and their songs are Dharma sounds which help him speak the Dharma.

Their clear and joyful sounds sound good to everyone. Everyone who hears them becomes happy because the sounds penetrate right into the heart. What is heard in the clear and joyful sounds? The sounds of the birds are the sounds of Dharma.

The Five Roots:

1. The root of faith,

2. The root of vigor,

3. The root of mindfulness,

4. The root of samadhi,

5. The root of wisdom.

The five roots germinate Bodhi seeds and cause your Bodhi heart to grow until it fully matures into...

The Five Powers:

1. The power of faith,

2. The power of vigor,

3. The power of mindfulness,

4. The power of samadhi,

5. The power of wisdom.

The Seven Bodhi Shares, also called the Seven Limbs of Enlightenment, are:

1. Selecting a dharma,

2. Vigorously cultivating it,

3. Joy, derived from cultivation,

4. Casting out coarse delusions,

5. Renouncing subtle delusions,

6. Samadhi,

7. Mindfulness.

These seven are very important and all Buddhist disciples should know them.

The Eight Sagely Way Shares, also known as the Proper Eight-fold Path, are:

1. Proper Views.

This refers to your manner of regarding something, your mental outlook and your opinions, not to what you view with your eyes. You practice the non-outflow conduct in contemplating yourself. Your own views and understanding must be proper. But you may also explain Proper Views as the view you see with your eyes, that is, you may view what is proper, but not what is improper.

Improper means "deviant," as when people see something that causes them to give rise to deviant thoughts. The "view" is one's vision of external manifestations. For example, if a Bhiksu sees an improper person, he should not continue to look at him; if he looks, that is called an improper view. The Sramanera Precepts say, "Don't sing or dance, use popular instruments, or attend or listen to such events." Improper thoughts are also improper views. But if you can "see without seeing," although it is improper, you don't think of it as such, you may then be said to have proper views.

2. Proper Thought.

Internally, where people cannot see, you use non-outflow wisdom. It is most important to be without outflows. I have explained this many times, but it seems that the more I explain it, the more outflows you have! Outflows flow out, you have a tiny bit of the water of wisdom, but you let it flow right out and use instead the fire of ignorance. There is nothing more wonderful in heaven and earth than the dharma-door of no-outflows, and yet you still take no notice of it. Even if Shakyamuni Buddha himself appeared, if you had outflows, he couldn't take you across.

To be without outflows, you must be free from improper knowledge, be without improper views and have no sexual desire. If you have sexual desire, you have outflows. With no sexual desire, you have no outflows. Just this is proper thought. If you have desire, you have outflows, if you have no desire, you have no outflows. Proper thoughts belong to the mind, do not give rise to evil thoughts in the mind.

3. Proper Speech.

With proper speech what you say is not the slightest bit off-color. Your speech is completely correct.

If someone speaks improperly to you, you should think of it as proper. This is pure mouth karma. Worldly men are of many kinds, and when they speak improperly, do not criticise them saying "Ah! He is speaking incorrectly!" On the other hand, be careful not to get too close to such people either. Proper thought is pure mind karma and proper speech is pure mouth karma.

4. Proper Action.

Proper action refers to pure bodily karma. Use non-outflow wisdom do discard improper bodily karma, specifically sexual desires. I can't make it *too* clear, I can't say it *too* frankly. Many people say, "Oh well, emptiness is form and form is emptiness," and they casually play around. This is improper action.

When you use non-outflow wisdom, your behaviour is never improper. People with improper wisdom are not intelligent enough to behave properly, but they can do evil things, things involving men and women, miraculously well, better than anyone else.

Proper action is purity of the body. Proper action, proper speech, proper thought mean purity of the karmas of body, mouth and mind.

5. Proper Livelihood.

Proper livelihood refers to any livelihood which does not fall within the five kinds of improper livelihood:

a) Manifesting a strange style. "Look at me," says the Great Vehicle monk dressed in Small Vehicle robes. "I am special. You should make offerings to me."

"He is special," say the blind followers. "He is probably a Buddha or a Bodhisattva," taking the gaudy rick-rack for a treasure.

b) Speaking of your own merit and virtue. "Do you know me? I have done many good deeds. I put a whole lot of money into building that bridge over there, and people walk back and forth on it because of my merit and virtue. I built a home for the aged and a school and I established scholarships as well. I built a temple where I support several hundred Dharma masters, and I am acting as their Dharma protector. The merit and virtue is mine – all mine!" They can get away with telling such stories to stupid people, but people with wisdom don't even have to hear what they are saying; they can tell by looking at them that they are just telling stories.

c) Fortune telling. People consult an oracle. "You should give me a million dollars," he says, "and do good deeds. If you don't, you will die tomorrow."

"A million dollars isn't too much to pay for my life," the victim thinks, and so he gives, and the next day he doesn't die. Of course he wouldn't have anyway, but still he believes that he might have.

"Tomorrow," says the fortune-teller, "a very lucky thing will happen if you do a good deed today. Give fifty pounds of gold today and tomorrow you will get five hundred."

"Ten to one is not a bad ratio," the man says handing him fifty pounds of gold. But the next day there is no gold, and he can't find the fortune-teller either! "And I thought I did met an immortal," he says.

d) Shouting and bragging. When it isn't necessary, why shout? A certain Dharma master used to startle people by bellowing at them. People were impressed even though they had no idea what he was saying. His voice was very resonant, but what is the point of yelling? With many people present, you can speak a little louder. Otherwise you shouldn't yell. Why does a Dharma master shout? He doesn't know that it is one of the five improper means of livelihood.

e) Speaking of your own offerings. "I had the best lunch at layman so and so's house," he says, reciting the "lunch mantra." "I had white fungus, mushrooms…"

Another layman hears the mantra and can't take it. "I did better borrow a hundred dollars and offer some vegetable to the Dharma master." He doesn't know that the Dharma master has transgressed the boundaries of proper livelihood by reciting the "lunch mantra" to move the layman's mind and obtain good offerings.

6. Proper Vigor.

This means bowing to the Buddha, reciting the Buddha's name from morning to night, without resting. Strangely enough, if you go to chat with someone, the more you chat, the more energy you have – talking, talking, too much talking. But of what use is all your vigorous talking? It is improper vigor.

Proper vigor means doing that which is beneficial, improper vigor involves doing that which is not beneficial, such as being lazy with respect to the Buddhadharma, but chatting more vigorously than anyone else. A person with proper vigor comes to listen to the sutras when they are being lectured, no matter how busy he is. One with improper vigor doesn't come, even though he has nothing else to do. Going to the movies, going sight-seeing, going everywhere but to the temple to listen to sutras is called improper vigor. Hunting for the best place to go gambling is also improper vigor.

7. Proper Samadhi.

Samadhi, a Sanskrit word, means "right reception,"[68] or "right concentration."[69] Use non-outflow wisdom to cultivate samadhi and no improper states will move you. If you could remember even one sentence of the sutras I have explained to you, then when the time comes you could use it. But you forget, and so you meet the state, are turned by it, and run after it. This is because you have no proper concentration, no proper samadhi.

"I know, I know," you say, "I know I don't have the proper samadhi."

If you know you don't have it, then why don't you find a way to obtain it? People! If you tell them that they have made a mistake, they say, "I know, I know." If they know, why do they make such mistakes?

8. Proper Mindfulness.

---

68. *zheng shou* 正受
69. *zheng ding* 正定

Be mindful of non-outflow wisdom. Do not have outflows. No matter what, don't indulge in the slightest sexual desire. Having no sexual desire is proper mindfulness. Any thoughts of sexual desire is improper mindfulness. Someone once said, "That person is attracted to me. I can tell by the look in his eyes."

If you didn't have sexual desire yourself, you wouldn't be looking into his eyes in the first place. Just what kind of thoughts are you having when you look into his eyes? If you didn't have sexual desire, you wouldn't know that he did. If you were clear, clear, pure, pure, spotless, and undefiled, how would you detect his desire? Speak up! If you know that others have desire, then you have it too, and, not having cut it off, your mindfulness is improper.

You may explain these Eight Sagely Way Shares any way you wish, as long as it is with principle. However, you can't just open your mouth and not know what to say. In explaining the Dharma you must speak correctly and not deviate from the principle in the least bit.

And dharmas such as these refers to the Four Applications of Mindfulness, the Five Roots, the Five Powers, the Seven Bodhi Shares, the Eight Sagely Way Shares, the Four Right Efforts, and the Four Bases of Supernatural Power – thirty-seven in all, the Thirty-seven Wings of Enlightenment.

The Four Right Efforts are:

1. Putting an end to evil which already exists.
2. Preventing evil not yet arisen from arising.
3. Bringing goodness which does not yet exist into existence.
4. Developing the good which already exists.

The Four Bases of Supernatural Power are:

1. Zeal,
2. Vigor,
3. Mindfulness,
4. Thought.

Sutra:

"Shariputra, do not say that these birds are born as retribution for their karmic offences. For what reason? In this Buddhaland there are no three evil ways of rebirth. Shariputra, in this Buddhaland not even the names of the three evil ways exist, how much the less their actuality! Desiring that the Dharma-sound be widely proclaimed, Amitabha Buddha by transformation made this multitude of birds.

Commentary:

Do not say that these birds came from one of the three evil realms. Why? In the Land of Ultimate Bliss there are not even the names of the hells, the realm of animals, or the realm of the hungry ghosts. How much the less could such creatures actually exist!

"Then where did the birds come from?"

Wishing to spread the Dharma-sound far and wide, with his vow power Amitabha created the kalavinkas and all the other birds to help him. They come from his spiritual penetrations and transformations, not from the three evil paths. Unlike the birds in this world which are born in the realms of animals, they are transformations of Amitabha Buddha's Dharma power.

Sutra:

"Shariputra, in that Buddhaland when the soft wind blows, the rows of jewelled trees and jewelled nets give forth subtle and wonderful sounds, like one hundred thousand kinds of music played at the same time. All those who hear these sounds naturally bring forth in their hearts mindfulness of the Buddha, mindfulness of the Dharma, and mindfulness of the Sangha.

"Shariputra, the realisation of the Land of Ultimate Bliss is thus meritoriously adorned.

Commentary:

"Shariputra," said Shakyamuni Buddha, "I'll tell you how it is in the Land of Ultimate Bliss. The gentle breezes blow through small bells hanging from the seven layers of netting on the seven rows of trees. Their sound helps us recollect the Buddha, the Dharma, and the Sangha and is like a hundred thousand kinds of subtle music playing harmoniously all at once. Those who hear these sounds have no defiled thoughts but instead naturally recite,

> *Namo Amitabha Buddha;*
> *Namo Amitabha Dharma;*
> *Namo Amitabha Sangha."*

You ask, "Namo Amitabha Buddha," perhaps, but how can they recite "Namo Amitabha Dharma?"

It's the Dharma which Amitabha Buddha taught, how can you not say "Namo Amitabha Dharma?" This is also the Sangha which Amitabha Buddha taught and transformed, so how can you not say, "Namo Amitabha Sangha?" Don't be so unimaginative. My explanation is a new explanation for an old meaning, just like my explanation of Nirvana:

> *"Nir" means "not produced" and*
> *"Vana" means "not destroyed."*
> *What is not produced? Sexual desire.*
> *What is not destroyed? Wisdom.*

In the realm of Nirvana, the Buddha has no sexual desire, he is clear, pure, and undefiled. He is without improper thoughts of desire. His self-nature constantly gives rise to wisdom which is never destroyed.

"Shariputra!" Shakyamuni Buddha called again. He is especially fond of his great disciple and thinks to himself, "Shariputra has a little wisdom, but he doesn't know what to ask. I will have to tell him."

Sutra:

"Shariputra, what do you think? Why is this Buddha called Amitabha? Shariputra, the brilliance of that Buddha's light is measureless, illumining the lands of the ten directions everywhere without obstruction, for this reason he is called Amitabha.

Commentary:

Shariputra should have asked this question himself, but just like you, he had gone off to samadhi. Whenever I ask you a question, you just stare at me blankly.

Why is this Buddha called Amitabha? Amitabha means "limitless light." This Buddha's light is immeasurable so that not a single land in the ten directions is screened from it. For this reason he is called Amitabha.

Sutra:

"Moreover, Shariputra, the life of that Buddha and that of his people extends for measureless, limitless asamkhyeya kalpas; for this reason he is called Amitayus. And Shariputra, since Amitabha realised Buddhahood ten kalpas have passed.

Commentary:

Asamkhyeya, a Sanskrit word, means "limitless number."[70] *Amitayus* means "limitless life." It's been ten great kalpas, or aeons, since he became a Buddha and how many great kalpas he will live in the future is uncertain, but boundless, measureless, asamkheyaya kalpas they will be.

---

70. *wu liang shu* 無量數

Sutra:

"Moreover, Shariputra, that Buddha has measureless, limitless 'sound-hearer' disciples, all Arhats, their number incalculable; thus also is the assembly of Bodhisattvas.

"Shariputra, the realisation of the Land of Ultimate Bliss is thus meritoriously adorned.

Commentary:

In Amitabha Buddha's Land of Ultimate Bliss, there are many Sravakas, "sound-hearer" disciples who have certified to the attainment of non-outflows and are all Arhats without desire. You can't count them. The assembly of Bodhisattvas is just as big.

Sutra:

"Moreover, Shariputra, those living beings born in the Land of the Ultimate Bliss are all avaivartika. Among them are many who in this very life will dwell in Buddhahood. Their number is extremely many; it is incalculable and only in measureless, limitless asamkhyeya kalpas could it be spoken.

Commentary:

Avaivartika is Sanskrit. It means "not retreating or turning away."[71] Those beings who are avaivartika do not retreat in position, conduct, or thought.

Not retreating in position means that they do not retreat to the lesser vehicle. Those of the lesser vehicle who are avaivartika do not retreat to the position of common men.

Not retreating in thought means that every day their thoughts to cultivate increase. Not retreating in conduct means that day by day they work harder and never say, "I have cultivated for quite a while,

---

71. *bu tui zhuan* 不退轉

it is time to take a rest." Taking a rest is simply retreating and turning away from *Annuttarasamyaksambodhi*, "the utmost right and perfect enlightenment." Those who are avaivartika do not retreat in their quest for Bodhi.

There are many living beings in the Land of Ultimate Bliss who in this very life can step into the position of Buddhahood. Born in a lotus flower, in one life they can realise Buddhahood. How many such beings are there? You could never count them all. They can't be calculated or even estimated. All you can say is that, in limitless, measureless asamkhyeya kalpas, you could not name them all.

Sutra:

"Shariputra, those living beings who hear should vow, 'I wish to be born in that country.' And why? Those who thus attain are all superior and good people, all gathered together in one place. Shariputra, one cannot have few good roots, blessings, virtues, and causal connections to attain birth in that land.

Commentary:

Shakyamuni Buddha said, "All those living beings who hear the doctrine I teach should vow to be born in the Land of Ultimate Bliss. Why? Because the Sravakas and Bodhisattvas born there are all superior and good people."

Although you may express the desire to be born in the Land of Ultimate Bliss, unless you have good roots, blessings, and virtuous conduct, you won't be able to be reborn there. You must have cultivated all the Paramita doors for many lifetimes and in this way obtained great good roots, great blessings, and great virtue, in order to have the opportunity to meet this wonderful Dharma.

Sutra:

"Shariputra, if there is a good man or a good woman who hears spoken 'Amitabha' and holds the name, whether

for one day, two days, three, four, five days, six days, as long as seven days, with one heart unconfused, when this person approaches the end of life, before him will appear Amitabha and all the assembly of holy ones. When the end comes, his heart is without inversion; in Amitabha's Land of Ultimate Bliss he will attain rebirth. Shariputra, because I see this benefit, I speak these words: If living beings hear this spoken they should make the vow, 'I will be born in that land.'

Commentary:

"Shariputra," said the Buddha, "if a good man or woman, that is one who holds the five precepts and cultivates the ten good deeds, hears the name 'Amitabha Buddha,' that person should hold to the recitation of Amitabha Buddha's name, just like holding something tightly in the hand." Recite the name, "Namo Amitabha Buddha, Namo Amitabha Buddha, Namo Amitabha Buddha…"

Whether for one day. In Chinese, the word "whether" looks like this: 若 (*ruo*). If you move the stroke in the middle, it changes into the word "suffering," which looks like this: 苦 (*ku*). So you could say, "*suffering* for one day, two days, three, four, five days, six days." If you recite the Buddha's name from four o'clock in the morning until ten at night for seven days, you can reach the level of **one heart unconfused**. When your life is about to end, Amitabha Buddha thinks, "That living being suffered for seven days reciting my name, and so now I will guide him to the Land of Ultimate Bliss. The time has come!" Then, Amitabha with Avalokitesvara Bodhisattva, Mahasthamaprapta Bodhisattva, and the entire clear, pure, ocean-wide assembly of Bodhisattvas appear before you, and lead you to the Land of Ultimate Bliss. If you think you can escape, you can't. You are surrounded. At this time, your heart is **without inversion**. You won't say, "I don't want to go! It's too boring there!" It would never occur to you to refuse Amitabha's invitation, and so you are born at once in the Western Land.

"Shariputra," the Buddha continues, "I see the advantages and so I am explaining them to you. If other living beings in the Saha world hear these doctrines, they should make the vow to be born in that land."

Previously, the text said, "Those living beings who hear should vow, 'I wish to be born in that country.'" This passage says, "I *will* be born in that land," that is "I vow that I shall certainly be born in the Land of Ultimate Bliss."

Sutra:

"**Shariputra, as I now praise the inconceivable benefit from the merit and virtue of Amitabha, thus in the east are also Aksobhya Buddha, Sumeru Appearance Buddha, Great Sumeru Buddha, Sumeru Light Buddha, Wonderful Sound Buddha, all Buddhas such as these, numberless as Ganges sands. In his own country each brings forth the appearance of a vast and long tongue, everywhere covering the three thousand great thousand worlds, and speaks the sincere and actual words, 'All you living beings should believe, praise, and hold in reverence the inconceivable merit and virtue of this sutra of the mindful one of whom all Buddhas are protective.'**

Commentary:

"Not only do I praise the subtle wonderful, inconceivable merit and virtue of Amitabha Buddha's beneficial deeds," said Shakyamuni Buddha, "but so does Aksobhya Buddha in the East."

Aksobhya Buddha of the Vajra division in the East is the Buddha who eradicates disaster and lengthens life. His name means, "unmoving and eternally dwelling Dharma body."[72] His Dharma body does not move, and it eternally dwells.

---

72. *bu dong fa shen chang zhu* 不動法身常住

Sumeru Appearance Buddha. Sumeru means "wonderfully high."[73] This Buddha's marks are as lofty as Mount Sumeru. **Great Sumeru Buddha**, that is, Great Wonderfully High Buddha. **Sumeru Light Buddha**, Wonderfully High Light Buddha. **All Buddhas such as these**. The names of a few of the Eastern Buddhas have been mentioned. If one were to speak of them in detail, they would be as **numberless as Ganges sands**.

In his own country, each brings forth the appearance of a vast and long tongue, everywhere covering the three thousand great thousand worlds. How can one speak with a tongue like that?

This represents the Buddhadharma circulating to all places, and the Buddha's sincere and actual words, "All of you should believe, praise, and hold in reverence, the inconceivable merit and virtue of **this sutra of the mindful one of whom all Buddhas are protective**." The Buddhas are mindful and protective of this sutra, just as they are mindful and protective of the *Wonderful Dharma Lotus Blossom Sutra*. If you read or recite the *Amitabha Sutra*, the Buddhas of the ten directions will happily come to your aid, and in the future, when your life is over, they will witness your rebirth in the Land of Ultimate Bliss.

Sutra:

"Shariputra, in the Southern world are Sun Moon Lamp Buddha, Well-known Light Buddha, Great Blazing Shoulders Buddha, Sumeru Lamp Buddha, Measureless Vigor Buddha, all Buddhas such as these, numberless as Ganges sands. In his own country each brings forth the appearance of a vast and long tongue, everywhere covering the three thousand great thousand worlds, and speaks the sincere and actual words, 'All you living beings should believe, praise, and hold in reverence the inconceivable

---

73. *miao gao* 妙高

merit and virtue of this sutra of the Mindful One of Whom all Buddhas are Protective.'

Commentary:

After speaking of the Buddhas in the East who praise Amitabha Buddha, Shakyamuni Buddha spoke of the Buddhas in the South. "Shariputra," he said, "in the South as well there are many, many Buddhas who extend their vast and long tongues to speak about the Dharma." Who are they?

They are **Sun Moon Lamp Buddha, Well-known Light Buddha, Great Blazing Shoulders Buddha,** who emits light from his shoulders, **Sumeru Lamp Buddha,** that is Wonderfully High Lamp Buddha, and **Measureless Vigor Buddha** who is energetic in the six periods of the day and night, as well as other Buddhas in number as grains of sand in the Ganges river. They all extend their vast and long tongues to cover the three thousand great thousand worlds and speak the truth, speak of what is, and do not speak falsely.

"All living beings," they say, "in all lands and all countries and in all the limitless worlds, should **believe, praise, and hold in reverence** the inconceivable merit and virtue of this sutra." You must bring forth hearts of real faith, real vows, and real practice. Praise the inconceivable merit and virtue of this sutra which Shakyamuni Buddha spoke without request. If you believe, accept, praise, and recite it, all the Buddhas will protect you. Resolve to revere Amitabha Buddha and the *Amitabha Sutra.*

Sutra:

"Shariputra, in the Western world are Measureless Life Buddha, Measureless Appearance Buddha, Measureless Curtain Buddha, Great Light Buddha, Great Brightness Buddha, Jewelled Appearance Buddha, Pure Light Buddha, all Buddhas such as these, numberless as Ganges sands. In his own country each brings forth the appearance of a vast and long tongue, everywhere covering the three thousand

great thousand worlds, and speaks the sincere and actual words, 'All you living beings should believe, praise, and hold in reverence the inconceivable merit and virtue of this Sutra of the Mindful One of Whom all Buddhas are Protective.'

Commentary:

After speaking of the Buddhas in the East and South who praise Amitabha Buddha, Shakyamuni Buddha spoke of the Buddhas in the West, for example **Measureless Life Buddha,** who is just Amitabha, the Buddha of Limitless Life. You would recognise him right away. However, there are many Buddhas who have the same name. Measureless Life Buddha might be Amitabha, the teacher in the Western Land of Ultimate Bliss, or it might be some other Buddha. It might be Amitabha Buddha or it might not be. What if it is? What if it isn't? Don't be attached one way or the other, because there really isn't any "is" or "is not." The Buddhadharma is just that wonderful.

Which "is"? Which "isn't"? Is and is not are *your* discriminations. For the Buddha there is one substance, one unity, and no division between this and that. The Buddha is identical with the Way, and each Buddha is identical with every other. Although all Buddhas are the same, they are each adorned with their own individual characteristics. In spite of the differing adornments, they are not like people who become jealous and obstruct each other saying, "Hey! How can you be so mean to me?" The Buddha has none of this. "You are just me," he says, "and I am just you, with no division." Why? Because the Buddha has attained the state of no-self, where "is" and "is not" are the same.

Those who wish to become Buddhas must not have discriminative thoughts, false thoughts, desires, or longings. They must have nothing at all. This is truly wonderful to the extreme. Do not be attached. If you actually recognise Amitabha Buddha, you won't waste your energy trying to discriminate one limitless life Buddha from another.

Measureless Appearance Buddha has limitless marks. It is not known how many Buddha-marks he has. **Measureless Curtain Buddha** is covered and sheltered by many jewelled curtains. **Great Light Buddha**'s light shines everywhere. **Great Brightness Buddha, Jewelled Appearance Buddha,** and **Pure Light Buddha,** all have a clear, pure, bright light. Were we to speak of all the Buddhas who are such as these in detail, they would be as numerous as the grains of sand in the Ganges river.

All the Buddhas in the Western Land of Ultimate Bliss and in the many Buddha-worlds extend their gigantic tongues. Now, when we extend our tongues, they can't even cover a room, but the tongues of the Buddhas cover the entire three thousand great thousand world systems. Why? For them, the three thousand great thousand world systems are just one thought, and one thought is just the three thousand great thousand worlds. Three thousand great thousand worlds are not beyond one thought, and the Buddha's tongue covers them all.

Don't be attached to the idea that the Buddha's tongue is actually that big. If it were, his speech would be clumsy. The appearance of the Buddha's vast and long tongue indicates that, wherever there is Dharma, the Buddha's tongue is there, too. It is not for certain that our tongues are small. We too, can extend our vast and long tongues and cover the three thousand great thousand worlds, speaking the Dharma and causing it to circulate.

When you hear the Buddhadharma, don't be attached. Although a tongue covers the three thousand great thousand worlds, there is not even a mote of dust; there is basically nothing at all.

"Nothing?" you ask. "Then was the Buddha lying?"

If the Buddha did not lie, how could you believe him! From the point of view of living beings, it seems to be a lie, but from the point of view of the Buddha, it is true, real speech, not false speech, not a lie. Living beings see it as a lie and the Buddha sees it as the truth. It's the same speech, but when the Buddha speaks it, it's true and when living beings speak it, it's a lie. This point is not easy to understand. If you want to be clear about this doctrine, do not fear suffering or difficulty. Work hard! You can't just study for two and a half days and then think that you have mastered the work. You can't stop listening to sutras or reciting the Buddha's name. Don't pretend to be investigating dhyana by doing nothing at all and saying, "I know what the Buddha said. There's not much to it, really. I have studied for about five years and it is all like that, not very interesting. So now I study nothing at all and it's a great improvement. I don't have nearly so many problems." Such talk is not very principled, wouldn't you say?

You should know that Shakyamuni Buddha cultivated blessings and wisdom for three asamkhyeya kalpas by practising giving and studying the Buddhadharma. He cultivated his fine characteristics for a hundred great kalpas and as a consequence he has the thirty two marks and eighty minor characteristics of a Buddha. Why don't we have a single mark? Why do people look at you and say, "He is so ugly. Keep away from him. He is no good, you can tell by looking at him?" Some people make you angry on sight. Why? It is because they don't cultivate and they have no virtuous conduct, and it shows up in their appearance.

The Buddha's tongue, then, covers the entire universe and speaks the truth. The Buddha does not cheat and he does not lie. Do not try to fathom the Sage's wisdom with your ordinary opinions; don't try to measure the Sage's mind with your common mind. Haven't I always told you that the first level Bodhisattvas don't know the realm of second level Bodhisattvas, and tenth level Bodhisattvas don't know the realm of equal enlightenment Bodhisattvas? First stage Arhats don't know the realms of second stage Arhats, and second stage Arhats don't know the realm of third stage Arhats. First stage Arhats may think that they are doing things correctly, but from the point of view of second stage Arhats they may be wrong. Second stage Arhats may think they are right, but the third stage Arhats may look at them and say, "You are off just a little bit."

I am your teacher, and you can't know my realm. If you knew, you wouldn't need a teacher. So reflect upon what I say. Don't complain, "He is just talking." This world is very dangerous. The only reason you haven't disintegrated in the sea of suffering is because the Buddhas and Bodhisattvas are protecting you.

Sutra:

"Shariputra, in the Northern world are Blazing Shoulders Buddha, Most Victorious Sound Buddha, Hard To Injure Buddha, Sun Birth Buddha, Net Brightness Buddha, all Buddhas such as these, numberless as Ganges sands. In his own country each brings forth the appearance of a vast and long tongue, everywhere covering the three thousand great thousand worlds, and speaks the sincere and actual words, 'All you living beings should believe, praise, and hold in reverence the inconceivable merit and virtue of this Sutra of the Mindful One of Whom all Buddhas are Protective.'

Commentary:

Not only are the Buddhas in the East, South and West are praising Amitabha Buddha, but those in the North praise him as well.

Great **Blazing Shoulders Buddha** emits light from his shoulders. **Most Victorious Sound Buddha** has a spectacular sound which is heard throughout the three thousand great thousand worlds.

"Then why haven't I heard it?" you ask.

You aren't in that world system of three thousand great thousand worlds. If you were, of course you would hear it. But you are in this world system, not that one.

Hard To Injure Buddha cannot be destroyed. No one can defame his Buddhadharma. You should hold in reverence the **inconceivable merit and virtue,** for it is most wonderful. Were the merit and virtue conceivable, it would have a limit. The sutra's merit and virtue is without a limit and so it is the **Sutra of the Mindful One of Whom all Buddhas are Protective**. Because its merit and virtue is very wonderful, it is the sutra of which all Buddhas are mindful and protective. Because it is a sutra of which all Buddha's are mindful and protective, its meritorious virtue is extremely wonderful.

Now I shall quit speaking and that is also wonderful. Were I to keep talking, it wouldn't be wonderful.

Sutra:

"**Shariputra, in the world below are Lion Buddha, Well-known Buddha, Famous Light Buddha, Dharma Buddha, Dharma Curtain Buddha, Dharma Maintaining Buddha, all Buddhas such as these, numberless as Ganges sands. In his own country each brings forth the appearance of a vast and long tongue, everywhere covering the three thousand great thousand worlds, and speaks the sincere and actual words, 'All you living beings should believe, praise, and hold in reverence the inconceivable merit and virtue of this Sutra of the Mindful One of Whom all Buddhas are Protective.'**

Commentary:

Having spoken of the Buddhas in the North, East, South, and West, Shakyamuni Buddha again says to Shariputra, "In the world below there is a Buddha named **Lion** who speaks the Dharma with a lion's roar."

Well-known Light Buddha's name has been heard by everyone in the triple world. **Famous Light Buddha**'s light as well as his fame shines everywhere within the triple world. **Dharma Curtain Buddha** has a jewelled Dharma curtain. **Dharma Maintaining Buddha** exclusively upholds the Buddhadharma. You can explain his name in two ways: The first is that there is such a Buddha in the world below; the second is that you who now receive, maintain, and recite the *Amitabha Sutra* will in the future become Dharma Maintaining Buddhas.

Sutra:

"Shariputra, in the world above are Pure Sound Buddha, King of Past Lives Buddha, Superior Fragrance Buddha, Fragrant Light Buddha, Great Blazing Shoulders Buddha, Vari-colored Jewels and Flower Adornment Body Buddha, Sala Tree King Buddha, Jewelled Flower Virtue Buddha, Vision of All Meaning Buddha, Such As Mount Sumeru Buddha, all Buddhas such as these, numberless as Ganges sands. In his own country each brings forth the appearance of a vast and long tongue, everywhere covering the three thousand great thousand worlds and speaks the sincere and actual words, 'All you living beings should believe, praise, and hold in reverence the inconceivable merit and virtue of this Sutra of the Mindful One of Whom all Buddhas are Protective.'

Commentary:

Pure Sound Buddha's sound is clear, pure, and resonant. **King of Past Lives Buddha** in past lives made great and powerful vows. If you light incense, **Superior Fragrance Buddha** will appear and **Fragrant Light Buddha** will emit light. As in the Southern world, in the world above there is also a Buddha called **Great Blazing Shoulders**. This light from his shoulders represents the two kinds of wisdom, provisional and real. **Vari-colored Jewels and Flower Adornment Body Buddha** adorns the virtue of his supreme attainment with the causal flowers of the ten thousand practices. **Sala Tree King Buddha**: the *Sala* tree is found in India. Sala means "solid and durable." No water can wash this tree away just as nothing can destroy the Buddha's Dharma body. The Buddha, then, is like the Sala tree.

Sutra:

"Shariputra, what do you think? Why is it called 'Sutra of the Mindful One of Whom all Buddhas are Protective?' Shariputra, if a good man or good woman hears this sutra and holds to it, and hears the names of all these Buddhas, this good man or woman will be the mindful one of whom all Buddhas are protective, and will irreversibly attain to anuttarasamyaksambodhi. Therefore, Shariputra, all of you should believe and accept my words and those which all Buddhas speak.

Commentary:

Having praised the Buddhas of the six directions, Shakyamuni Buddha asks, "Shariputra, in your opinion, why is this sutra called the 'Sutra of the Mindful One of Whom all Buddhas are Protective?'" This section of the sutra, then, discusses the sutra's name.

Shariputra just stared blankly. Shakyamuni Buddha waited in silence for about five minutes, and then he said, "I will tell you. Shariputra, if there is a **good man** or a **good woman**, one who maintains the five precepts and cultivates the ten good deeds, who can receive, maintain, recite from memory, and not forget the names of the Buddhas just mentioned, that good man or woman will be **the Mindful One of Whom all Buddhas are Protective**. Not only will the Buddhas of the six directions come to his aid, but the Buddhas of all ten directions will support him. He will further attain to irreversibility of position, thought, and conduct with respect to the attainment of the utmost right and perfect enlightenment, anuttarasamyaksambodhi.

Therefore, Shariputra, all of you should believe and accept my words and those which all Buddhas speak. Do you see how extremely compassionate the Buddha is? We should be grateful to the point of tears and pay attention when the Buddha says, "All of you, adults and children as well, should believe and accept what I tell you."

You should also believe and accept what I explain to you now. Don't have doubts. Don't say, "When it comes right down to it, I don't know if the Chinese dharma master's doctrines are correct." You should believe what I say. You should also believe what Shakyamuni Buddha says and what all the Buddhas praise as **the inconceivable merit and virtue of this Sutra of the Mindful One of Whom all Buddhas are Protective**. Believe me when I say that this sutra's doctrines are true, real, and not false. You are certainly not being cheated, so vow to be born in the Land of Ultimate Bliss.

Sutra:

> **"Shariputra, if there are people who have already made the vow, who now make the vow, or who are about to make the vow, 'I desire to be born in Amitabha's Country,' these people, whether born in the past, now being born, or to be born in the future, all will irreversibly attain to anutt- arasamyaksambodhi. Therefore, Shariputra, all good men and good women, if they are among those who have faith, should make the vow, 'I will be born in that country.'**

Commentary:

There sat Shariputra, sound asleep!

"Shariputra! Shariputra! Wake up!" said the Buddha. "Those who have already vowed to be born in the Land of Ultimate Bliss have most certainly been born there. Those who now vow to be born there, and those who make the vow in the future will be born there in the future." But in order to make vows you must have faith. Faith, vows, and practice are the three prerequisites for cultivation of the Pure Land Dharma Door. First, believe there is a Land of Ultimate Bliss. Secondly, have faith in Amitabha Buddha. Thirdly, believe that you and Amitabha Buddha have a great karmic affinity, and that you can certainly be born in the Land of Ultimate Bliss.

With faith in these three things, you may then make the vow, "**I desire to be born in Amitabha's country.**" There is a saying,

"I want to be born in the Pure Western Land."

"I *want* to be born there. Nobody's forcing me to go, nobody's dragging me there. Although Amitabha Buddha has come to guide me, I am going as a volunteer because I want to be close to him. I want to be born in the Land of Ultimate Bliss and to see Amitabha Buddha when my lotus flower opens. I want to meet the Buddha and hear the Dharma." These are the vows you need.

Then you must practice. How? Recite the Buddha's name, saying "Namo Amitabha Buddha, Namo Amitabha Buddha..." as if you were trying to save your head from the executioner, running ahead to keep your head, like the Sixth Patriarch. He knew that after his death someone would try to steal his head, and so he told his disciples to take precautions. When he died, they wrapped his neck with sheets of iron. When the thief tried to cut off his head, he couldn't do it. The Great Master the Sixth Patriarch protected his head, even after he had entered the stillness of Nirvana. How much the more should we who have not entered the stillness "protect our heads" by cultivating the recitation of the Buddha's name. Reciting the Buddha's name is actual practice.

Faith, vows, and practice are the travel expenses for rebirth in the Land of Ultimate Bliss. They are your ticket.

All those who vow to be born in the Land of Ultimate Bliss can attain irreversible position, thought, and conduct with respect to the utmost right and perfect enlightenment. All those who believe should make the vow – and this is an order! No kidding around. **"I will be born in that country."** If you make this vow, you can be born in the Land of Ultimate Bliss.

Sutra:

"Shariputra, just as I now praise the inconceivable merit and virtue of all Buddhas, all those Buddhas equally praise my inconceivable merit and virtue saying these words, 'Shakyamuni Buddha can complete extremely rare and difficult deeds. In the Saha land, in the evil time of the five

turbidities, in the midst of the kalpa turbidity, the view turbidity, the affliction turbidity, the living beings turbidity, and the life turbidity, he can attain anuttarasamyaksambodhi and for the sake of living beings, speak this Dharma which in the whole world is hard to believe.'

Commentary:

"Shariputra," said the Buddha, "I will tell you some more good news. As I now praise the Buddhas in the six directions and the inconceivable merit and virtue of this sutra, all the Buddhas also praise me and my inconceivable merit and virtue."

"Shakyamuni Buddha," they say, "**can complete extremely rare and difficult deeds**. He's truly outstanding, truly rare. Why? He can do what men cannot do, deeds which are extremely rare and wonderful."

Shakya means "able to be humane," and *muni* means "still and silent." The Buddha humanely teaches and converts living beings, and silently returns the light within to cultivate samadhi. The humaneness is movement and the silence is stillness. He moves and yet is always still. He accords with conditions and yet never changes. For him there is nothing conditioned, nothing unconditioned, nothing done and nothing left undone. Shakyamuni Buddha is inconceivable.

In the Saha world, where one enjoys no bliss but endures every kind of suffering, living beings endure a great deal. They undergo the bitterness unaware that they are suffering.

In the evil time of the five turbidities. There are five turbidities in the Saha world and they are just terrible! The reason we don't realise Buddhahood is because we are stuck in the five turbidities, as if in quicksand, and can't pull ourselves out. When we lift one leg, the other leg sinks deeper, and when we lift that leg, the first goes down. There's really no escape.

But Shakyamuni Buddha is talented. With his great spiritual powers he can teach you to leap right out of the five turbidities, in a *ksana*, a mere instant of time. At night, when we recite the Great Transference of Merit, we say, "Leaving the five turbidities in a ksana, and arriving at the lotus pool in the flick of a wrist." Like a talented magician, Shakyamuni Buddha leaves the five turbidities, which are:

1. The kalpa turbidity.

Kalpa, that is, time, is turbid. It arises dependent upon the four other turbidities which increase daily, growing bigger and more extreme. That is to say, the turbidity of time is created with the help of the view turbidity, the affliction turbidity, the living beings turbidity, and the life turbidity, and takes the growth of the first four as its basic substance. It takes unceasing flaming as its mark, for, like flaming fuel, the more it burns, the higher it blazes.

2. The view turbidity.

The view turbidity takes the five quick servants as it's basic substance. The five quick servants are the view of a body, the view of extremes, deviant views, the view of grasping at views, and the view of prohibitive morality. It takes mistaken wisdom and cattle morality as its mark. Seeing a dog, a cat, or a cow reborn in the heavens, some people imitate their conduct so that they may be reborn there too. With deviant knowledge and views, they take the genuine doctrine to extremes.

3. The affliction turbidity.

The affliction turbidity takes the five dull servants, greed, hatred, stupidity, pride and doubt, as it's basic substance, and the irritation of afflictions as it's mark.

4. The living beings turbidity.

The living beings turbidity takes the combination of the three conditions of father, mother, and one's own karma as it's basic substance. It takes the unceasing turning of the wheel of rebirth as its mark. After the three conditions combine, the wheel revolves without stopping, back and forth. This life you are named John and next life, Lee. This life you are a bhiksu and next life you are a bhiksuni. Bhiksus become bhiksunis and bhiksunis turn into bhiksus. Isn't this amazing? It really is!

5. The life turbidity.

The life turbidity takes the reception of warmth as its basic substance and the decline and extinction of the life span as it's mark. From youth to middle age on to old age and death – this is the mark of life.

Sutra:

"Shariputra, you should know that I, in the evil time of the five turbidities, practice these difficult deeds, attain anuttarasamyaksambodhi, and for all the world speak this Dharma, difficult to believe, extremely difficult!"

The Transmission

Sutra:

After the Buddha spoke this sutra, Shariputra and all the bhiksus, all the gods, men, and asuras, and others from all the worlds, hearing what the Buddha had said, joyously welcomed, faithful accepted, bowed and withdrew.

End of the Buddha Speaks of Amitabha Sutra.

Commentary:

You should know that, in the midst of the five turbidities, Shakyamuni Buddha attains the utmost right and perfect enlightenment and then speaks about the Dharma which people find very difficult to believe. "This Dharma is most difficult to believe, extremely difficult, really hard to believe," says Shakyamuni Buddha.

Shakyamuni Buddha says it's hard, but I say it's easy. Shakyamuni Buddha just *said* it's hard. It's not hard, really. All you need to do is recite, "Namo Amitabha Buddha." Just go ahead and recite. Wouldn't you say that is easy? No trouble at all. It doesn't cost a thing and it takes no effort or time. It's an extremely easy Buddhadharma.

After the Buddha spoke the *Amitabha Sutra*, the greatly wise Shariputra and all the great bhiksus, all the world with its gods and men, as well as the eight classes of supernatural beings – gods, dragons, yaksa ghosts, gandharvas, asuras, garudas, kinnaras and mahoragas – **hearing what the Buddha had said, joyously welcomed, faithfully accepted, bowed and withdrew**. They bowed reverently to Shakyamuni Buddha to thank him for speaking the *Amitabha Sutra*, and for teaching and transforming living beings. At that time all the great Arhats bowed to the Buddha out of gratitude for having heard this Dharma.

We now, hearing this supreme, deep, subtle, and wonderful Dharma, have certainly planted great good roots in ages past. Consequently, we have a great affinity with Amitabha Buddha, and as a result have been fortunate enough to hear the *Amitabha Sutra* and to recite the Buddha's name. This is very rare.

Index

Buddhist Text Translation Society Publication

Buddhist Text Translation Society
International Translation Institute

http://www.bttsonline.org

1777 Murchison Drive,
Burlingame, California 94010-4504 USA
Phone: 650-692-5912 Fax: 650-692-5056

When Buddhism first came to China from India, one of the most important tasks required for its establishment was the translation of the Buddhist scriptures from Sanskrit into Chinese. This work involved a great many people, such as the renowned monk National Master Kumarajiva (fifth century), who led an assembly of over 800 people to work on the translation of the Tripitaka (Buddhist canon) for over a decade. Because of the work of individuals such as these, nearly the entire Buddhist Tripitaka of over a thousand texts exists to the present day in Chinese.

Now the banner of the Buddha's Teachings is being firmly planted in Western soil, and the same translation work is being done from Chinese into English. Since 1970, the Buddhist Text Translation Society (BTTS) has been making a paramount contribution toward this goal. Aware that the Buddhist Tripitaka is a work of such magnitude that its translation could never be entrusted to a single person, the BTTS, emulating the translation assemblies of ancient times, does not publish a work until it has passed through four committees for primary translation, revision, editing, and certification. The leaders of these committees are Bhikshus (monks) and Bhikshunis (nuns) who have devoted their lives to the study and practice of the Buddha's teachings. For this reason, all of the works of the BTTS put an emphasis on what the principles of the Buddha's teachings mean in terms of actual practice and not simply hypothetical conjecture.

The translations of canonical works by the Buddhist Text Translation Society are accompanied by extensive commentaries by the Venerable Tripitaka Master Hsuan Hua.

BTTS Publications

Buddhist Sutras. Amitabha Sutra, Dharma Flower (Lotus) Sutra, Flower Adornment (Avatamsaka) Sutra, Heart Sutra & Verses without a Stand, Shurangama Sutra, Sixth Patriarch Sutra, Sutra in Forty-two Sections, Sutra of the Past Vows of Earth Store Bodhisattva, Vajra Prajna Paramita (Diamond) Sutra.

Commentarial Literature. Buddha Root Farm, City of 10 000 Buddhas Recitation Handbook, Filiality: The Human Source, Herein Lies the Treasure-trove, Listen to Yourself Think Everything Over, Shastra on the Door to Understanding the Hundred Dharmas, Song of Enlightenment, The Ten Dharma Realms Are Not Beyond a Single Thought, Venerable Master Hua's Talks on Dharma, Venerable Master Hua's Talks on Dharma during the 1993 Trip to Taiwan, Water Mirror Reflecting Heaven.

Biographical. In Memory of the Venerable Master Hsuan Hua, Pictorial Biography of the Venerable Master Hsü Yün, Records of High Sanghans, Records of the Life of the Venerable Master Hsüan Hua, Three Steps One Bow, World Peace Gathering, News from True Cultivators, Open Your Eyes Take a Look at the World, With One Heart Bowing to the City of 10 000 Buddhas.

Children's Books. Cherishing Life, Human Roots: Buddhist Stories for Young Readers, Spider Web, Giant Turtle, Patriarch Bodhidharma.

Musics, Novels and Brochures. Songs for Awakening, Awakening, The Three Cart Patriarch, City of 10 000 Buddhas Color Brochure, Celebrisi's Journey, Lots of Time Left.

The Buddhist Monthly–Vajra Bodhi Sea is a monthly journal of orthodox Buddhism which has been published by the Dharma Realm Buddhist Association, formerly known as the Sino-American Buddhist Association, since 1970. Each issue contains the most recent translations of the Buddhist canon by the Buddhist Text Translation Society. Also included in each issue are a biography of a great Patriarch of Buddhism from the ancient past, sketches of the lives of contemporary monastics and lay-followers around the world, articles on practice, and other material. The journal is bilingual, Chinese and English

Please visit our web-site at **www.bttsonline.org** for the latest publications and for ordering information.

Dharma Realm Buddhist Association Branches

The City of Ten Thousand Buddhas
P.O. Box 217, Talmage, CA 95481-0217 USA
Tel: (707) 462-0939   Fax: (707) 462-0949
Home Page: http://www.drba.org

Institute for World Religions (Berkeley Buddhist Monastery)
2304 McKinley Avenue, Berkeley, CA 94703 USA
Tel: (510) 848-3440

Dharma Realm Buddhist Books Distribution Society
11th Floor, 85 Chung-hsiao E. Road, Sec. 6, Taipei, Taiwan R.O.C.
Tel: (02) 2786-3022   Fax: (02) 2786-2674

The City of the Dharma Realm
1029 West Capitol Avenue, West Sacramento, CA 95691 USA
Tel: (916) 374-8268

Gold Mountain Monastery
800 Sacramento Street, San Francisco, CA 94108 USA
Tel: (415) 421-6117   Fax: (415) 788-6001

Gold Wheel Monastery
235 North Avenue 58, Los Angeles, CA 90042 USA
Tel: (323) 258-6668

Gold Buddha Monastery
248 East 11th Avenue, Vancouver, B.C. V5T 2C3 Canada
Tel: (604) 709-0248   Fax: (604) 684-3754

Gold Summit Monastery
233 1st Avenue, West Seattle, WA 98119 USA
Tel: (206) 284-6690   Fax: (206) 284-6918

Gold Sage Monastery
11455 Clayton Road, San Jose, CA 95127 USA
Tel: (408) 923-7243   Fax: (408) 923-1064

The International Translation Institute
1777 Murchison Drive, Burlingame, CA 94010-4504 USA
Tel: (650) 692-5912   Fax: (650) 692-5056

Long Beach Monastery
3361 East Ocean Boulevard, Long Beach, CA 90803 USA
Tel: (562) 438-8902

Blessings, Prosperity, & Longevity Monastery
4140 Long Beach Boulevard, Long Beach, CA 90807 USA
Tel: (562) 595-4966

Avatamsaka Hermitage
11721 Beall Mountain Road, Potomac, MD 20854-1128 USA
Tel: (301) 299-3693

Avatamsaka Monastery
1009 4th Avenue, S.W. Calgary, AB T2P OK8 Canada
Tel: (403) 234-0644 Email: ava@nucleus.com

Kun Yam Thong Temple
161, Jalan Ampang, 50450 Kuala Lumpur, Malaysia
Tel: (03) 2164-8055 Fax: (03) 2163-7118

Prajna Guanyin Sagely Monastery (formerly Tze Yun Tung)
Batu 5½, Jalan Sungai Besi,
Salak Selatan, 57100 Kuala Lumpur, Malaysia
Tel: (03) 7982-6560 Fax: (03) 7980-1272

Lotus Vihara
136, Jalan Sekolah, 45600 Batang Berjuntai,
Selangor Darul Ehsan, Malaysia
Tel: (03) 3271-9439

Buddhist Lecture Hall
31 Wong Nei Chong Road, Top Floor, Happy Valley, Hong Kong, China
Tel: (02) 2572-7644

Dharma Realm Sagely Monastery
20, Tong-hsi Shan-chuang, Hsing-lung Village, Liu-kuei
Kaohsiung County, Taiwan, R.O.C.
Tel: (07) 689-3717 Fax: (07) 689-3870

Amitabha Monastery
7, Su-chien-hui, Chih-nan Village, Shou-feng,
Hualien County, Taiwan, R.O.C.
Tel: (07) 865-1956 Fax: (07) 865-3426

Verse of Transference

May the merit and virtue accrued from this work,
Adorn the Buddhas' Pure Lands,
Repaying four kinds of kindness above,
And aiding those suffering in the paths below.

May those who see and hear of this,
All bring forth the resolve for Bodhi,
And when this retribution body is over,
Be born together in the Land of Ultimate Bliss.

Dharma Protector Wei Tuo Bodhisattva